W9-CKY-435

Praise for *Missing Persons*

"A spiritual journey"

"Bruce Piasecki has added his own twist to the endlessly repeatable tale of self-invention, tracking a spiritual journey through love and faith, family and friends. *Missing Persons* is a book about the absences that define our lives, the tears in the fabric that we spend a lifetime trying to repair."

–Jay Parini
Author of *The Last Station*

"An inspiring read"

"What we first forget and then rescue from our memories make for the best memoirs. Bruce Piasecki, remembering in *Missing Persons*, inspires everyone to find what is missing in their own life. An inspiring read."

–Rabbi Laurence Aryeh Alpern
Temple Shabbat Shalom
Saratoga Springs, NY

"Eloquent"

"In this eloquent memoir Bruce Piasecki . . . celebrates the family and friends who made possible his journey from an impoverished childhood to hard earned success."

–Lucien Ross Tharaud
Contract Lawyer, Legal Editor

"Poignant and profound"

"Bruce Piasecki's memoir is a work of art—
lyrical and luminous . . . a moving account of the
people in his life who inspired him. From dirt poor
to best-selling author, Bruce never stops thinking
and feeling. It is a rare treat to reflect with him on
his journey. Poignant and profound."

–Sanford Schram
Professor of Political Science and Public Policy
Hunter College, CUNY

"Powerful"

"How do the street smarts learned at an
early age show a born poet and scholar the way
to wealth based on 'doing more with less?'
In a constantly surprising series of vignettes
based on love, labor, and loss, the protean
Bruce Piasecki has written a fable for our times,
one that reminds us of how powerful the art
of ordering our memories can prove. Meet here
a Ben Franklin for our times."

–R. Laurence Moore
Author of *Religious Outsiders*
and the Making of Americans

"With magic and surprise"

"Bruce Piasecki's lovely book *Missing Persons* reminds us that life does not just happen to us. Instead, it demonstrates how life responds to us with magic and surprise!"

–Erol User
CEO Founder Erol Corporation
Istanbul Turkey

"A sense of wonder"

"Bruce Piasecki's writing style possesses a sense of wonder that reaches a new level of imaginative discourse. Here, the magical realism and sensitivity to the people who have shaped his life bring a new understanding of this man, who has already done so much in the realms of business and life."

–Thaddeus Rutkowski
Author of *Haywire*

"A generosity of spirit"

"A delicious read! *Missing Persons* reveals the man behind business bestsellers like *Doing More With Less.* Piasecki's evocative vignettes reflect a generosity of spirit and a genuine humility that will inspire you to reflect on your own influences."

–William M. Throop
Professor of Philosophy and Environmental Studies
Green Mountain College

OTHER TITLES BY BRUCE PIASECKI

America's Future in Toxic Waste Management

Beyond Dumping

Corporate Environmental Strategy

Corporate Strategy Today

Doing More With Less

Doing More With Teams

Environmental Management and Business Strategy

In Search of Environmental Excellence

New World Companies

Stray Prayers

The Surprising Solution

World, Inc.

MISSING PERSONS

A Life of Unexpected Influences

BRUCE PIASECKI

SQUAREONE
PUBLISHERS

COVER DESIGNER: Jeannie Tudor
EDITOR: Peter Lynch
TYPESETTER: Gary A. Rosenberg
ARTWORK ON PAGES 56, 143, 154: Colette Piasecki-Masters
PHOTOGRAPHS ON PAGES 38, 41: Eugene Madsen

Square One Publishers
115 Herricks Road
Garden City Park, NY 11040
(516) 535-2010 • (877) 900-BOOK
www.squareonepublishers.com

The excerpt on page 141 is from "The Joy of Old Age. (No Kidding.)"
by Oliver Sacks. Copyright © 2013 by Oliver Sacks. Originally appeared
in *The New York Times*, used by permission of The Wylie Agency, LLC.

Library of Congress Cataloging-in-Publication Data
Piasecki, Bruce–
  Missing persons : a life of unexpected influences / Bruce Piasecki.
     pages cm
  ISBN 978-0-7570-0412-4 (quality pbk.)
1. Piasecki, Bruce, 1955—Family   2. Energy consultants—Biography.
3. New York (State)—Biography. I. Title.
  CT275.P598A3 2014
  974.7092—dc23
  [B]
                                                    2014033621

Contents

PART ONE

The Discovery of Colette

VIGNETTES OF INNOCENCE AND YOUTH

PART TWO

The Sensual Middle

VIGNETTES OF EXPERIENCE AND MIDDLE AGE

PART THREE

At Old Stone Church

VIGNETTES OF THE MAGIC IN OLD AGE

FINALE

This book of vignettes
I dedicate to the memory of
my mother and father,
and to my lovely wife
and loving daughter.

Acknowledgments

There are so many thanks due my lifelong readers and friends.

T.S. Eliot, in his lasting essay "The Function of Criticism," sums up my predicament in writing this eleventh book, when he notes that "only the man who has so much to give that he can forget himself in his work can afford to collaborate, to exchange, to contribute."

I was given so much by Sandy Chizinsky, my friend from Cornell and the owner of Beacon Editorial, who assisted me during the developmental phases of my last three books. Sandy is a muse to me, my second voice. In my collaboration with Sandy, and in my exchanges with my former Sourcebooks editor Peter Lynch, I was blessed with professional "word people" who already knew my strengths and weaknesses from my nonfiction books. Thanks in part to them, this project went from diary writing to a book perhaps worth sharing, maybe even worth keeping.

Additional substantive contributors to this effort include Karen Wallingford, founder of Wildwood Publicity; retired English teacher (and good friend) Barbara Kass; and my company's webmaster, Frank Weaver, of Aplomb Communications.

This manuscript also attracted early reads from many people—Rabbi Laurence Aryeh Alpern; a local priest who wishes to remain anonymous; two friends who are psychologists; six renowned editors from Manhattan's dominant publishers from

Farrar, Straus, and Giroux to Henry Holt, Penguin, and Simon and Schuster. Eugene Madsen, a soil ecologist and member of Cornell's distinguished agriculture faculty (who also happens to be the gymnast who first taught me how to stand on my head without a wall), and Alan Maikels, who has for over thirty years been my firm's accountant of record, read this manuscript and offered useful comments.

Most importantly, Ross Tharaud—my lawyer-painter-poet friend and soul-mate—used my completion of this manuscript as an opportunity to tell me how he had risen to my defense back in 1976 during a debate about *Stray Prayers*, my book of poetry. Ross, thanks for allowing me to start.

At my fortieth high school reunion, I read early drafts of these vignettes to fellow classmates—including Amy Williams, Pat Johnson, Patricia Eisemann, Patricia Rodman, and my great basketball teammates Guy Pelling and Marty Rolnick. They emerged smiling. Some embraced me for having captured the essence of my generous mother in their memories, and several wept while reflecting on the recent death of our great teacher Charles Plumer.

My 1990 Simon and Schuster editor, André Bernard—a writer himself—gave me help and encouragement during the dog days of this book, as did my alert and kind cousin Steven Kureczko, who nicknamed me "Cousin Big Head" so long ago.

What more can one ask as one turns sixty?

Writing brings you places—some magical, some simply inane—that you never expected to go. Many nonwriters can't imagine where a writer travels in the act of writing creatively about his own life. It is a lonely but majestic path, offering silent glory and a rare chance to make sense of it all. I do not recommend personal narratives to everyone, but it proved illuminating for me.

I am indeed lucky, not only for having grown up in the enveloping warmth of my multiracial family, but also for all my friends and readers—the makers of my life, in a sense, and the foundation of *Missing Persons*. Many thanks to Marie Caratozzolo, my in-house editor, and to the owner of Square One, Rudy Shur, the most devoted of publishers. Without Rudy, this would have remained a manuscript in my personal archives, and a book in hiding.

Once you read these vignettes, you'll sense the obvious: namely, that my deepest thanks are due to my daughter and wife. I love you both. Any heaviness or weaknesses are attributable to my own stubbornness and this bold trespass into creative writing.

Foreword

by Jay Parini

Missing Persons is an eye-opener both for its frankness and for how it fits yet distorts literary traditions.

I have endorsed Bruce Piasecki's prior nonfiction books. They are works of nonfiction with plenty of narrative skill in their rendering. But *Missing Persons* explores new territories by diving straight into the realms of poetry, psychology, self-invention, prosperity, personal narrative and the fate of families. This is the stuff of autobiography writ large, as I learned from editing the *Norton Anthology of American Autobiography.*

Throughout, Piasecki takes us on an unexpected journey into a new form of autobiography, a life story projected and reflected. For *Missing Persons* proves itself to have deep roots in American and in the Latin American traditions of magical realism. Furthermore, the author overall creates an atmosphere of pragmatic self-awareness. This comes directly from the realms of modern business, but also indirectly from the wit and ambitions of Ben Franklin. It is this eclectic mix that proves electrifying.

Jay Parini is a noted writer and Professor of English at Middlebury College in Vermont. He is the author of distinguished books of poetry; biographies of Robert Frost, John Steinbeck, and Jesus Christ; as well as a number of novels. He also edited the *Norton Anthology of American Autobiography.* Jay's historical novel *The Last Station* was made into an Academy Award-nominated film starring Helen Mirren.

Before you dive in, perhaps you'd find this useful to frame your expectations. For any judicious review of literature will suggest that autobiography lies at the dead center of the American enterprise—not a surprising fact, given that American history presupposes a radical sense of equality, one in which the individual is celebrated.

Walt Whitman's "Song of Myself" is truly our national anthem, although the self that Whitman celebrates moves well beyond petty individualism: this is the song of the American self, the common man who becomes, through awareness, education, and hard work, a distinct part of a larger whole.

As a distinct genre, autobiography was pioneered by Ben Franklin, the father of the form in its American incarnation, which is always the story of how a boy from nowhere cobbled together a life, found his footing in the world, and transformed that world along with himself, making himself part and parcel of a peculiar universe, one of his own self-invention. The genre migrates through various narrative modes, such as the journey of Henry David Thoreau to the edge of the village, where he builds a house of self on the shores of Walden Pond and discovers the universe. It reaches through the immigrant narratives of figures such as Mary Antin, who in *The Promised Land* put forward a paradigm of assimilation that has inspired generations of arrivals to these shores. It snakes through the narratives of Frederick Douglass and W.E.B. Du Bois, who framed the debate over race in America for all time, and moves through such great contemporary classics as Hemingway's *A Moveable Feast* or Annie Dillard's gorgeous *Pilgrim at Tinker Creek*. The genre seems endlessly protean, open to fresh voices and forms, expansive.

Bruce Piasecki has added his own twist to the endlessly repeatable tale of self-invention, tracking a spiritual journey through love and faith, family and friends. *Missing Persons* is a book about the absences that define our lives, the tears in the fabric that we spend a lifetime trying to repair. It's about what the poet Elizabeth Bishop called "The Art of Losing," and yet each loss foretells a gain, as Piasecki reshapes his life, rediscovers lost family and friends, and connects to literary ancestors—some of whom, like Walt Whitman, lend a layer of texture and allusion to his prose that makes it not only readable but re-readable.

As an ex-basketball player, Piasecki does not presume he can jump as high as Ben Franklin or Whitman or Jonathan Edwards or Casanova, just a few of the writers he channels. Instead, in an unpretentious, tactical, and sure-footed way, he examines the events that shaped his own life through the lens of these great writers, inhabiting what he calls the "neighborhood" of their lives. Their books are his neighbors and friends throughout this memoir, and he echoes them at every turn.

Missing Persons includes over seventy interrelated vignettes—tiny nuggets of narration that nest within the larger narrative arc as the author describes his growing self-awareness, a slowly widening sense of the world. The vignettes move in a roughly chronological fashion, but some of them play back and repeat certain themes and motifs—as with key characterizations of the author's long dead father, Walter, his generous mother Lillian, his lovely daughter Colette, and his strong wife Varlissima. These characters dance in his head, and their voices underpin his own. They appear and disappear, flash and fade.

Piasecki is a natural postmodernist, and he plays easily—one might almost say fast and loose—with time, as in the final section, where he writes the autobiography of his future. He builds on understandings already attained, while shaping a larger understanding of his own selfhood in response to the world. Indeed, this is a work of fiction in the truest sense. That is, it's about creating narratives by highlighting some themes, hiding others. As the author dances around the absences in his life, he uses language itself—a supple instrument in his hands—to create new wholes, to fill spaces, to make a life of ampleness and plenitude.

This is a fresh and highly readable contribution to the art of autobiography. It has narrative thrills and the *frissons* of poetic insights. By accretion and artful juxtaposition, the author builds a life. But *Missing Persons* is not just a reflection on the life of Bruce Piasecki, businessman and scholar, entrepreneur and family man.

Piasecki becomes, in effect, every man here, dramatizing the sorrows and joys that come into our lives, taking us through his experiences, allowing us to enter his world in ways that become our world, as readers.

Preface

I started writing *Missing Persons* on the day my daughter, Colette, was born, in late August of 1996, not far from the Northern Kingdom of the Adirondacks. "The Discovery of Colette" was the first vignette that came to mind. This two-page prose poem was sparked by the simple joy of bringing a daughter into the world. It had no other purpose but to express that joy.

Some years later, I found myself struggling to confront the pain I had felt since the death of my father, when I was three years old. That pain was soon compounded in 2009 by the loss of my mother. With Lillian's death, I realized that in all likelihood, I would die before Colette turned forty-two—the age I had been when she was born. In attempting to sort through these losses, I found it easier—and somehow more honest—to write in the third person. This approach helped me to fight through the fog of lived experience by "reading through" my own life.

I now thank you for your attention. Of the books I have written to date, this was the hardest—and I wondered at times whether I should even release this text into the world. I now ask for your indulgence. I did need to change the names of some of the characters—both to protect their privacy and to enable them to warm to this project. Personal narrative can easily taint friendships and disrupt love.

When Rudy Shur, publisher and owner of Square One Publishers, offered to buy a backlist of my business books and include a "creative piece based on lived experiences" in the series, I begged him to keep the pattern and sequence of the vignette format. Today's reader expects more than embellished, expository prose: authors must re-earn the reader's attention on nearly every other page.

This brings me to the next reason I seek your indulgence: this book is a product of memory and creativity, not of chronology and fact. Does not all memory reshape event and thought, family and friends? And are not shared memories much larger than identity? In telling the truth of my life, I had to ask myself these hard questions.

As I thought about the films I've loved, from Federico Fellini's *La Strada* to James Cameron's *Avatar,* I realized that I wanted to write in color, and to explore a more cinematic approach to prose. After all, the new generation of readers is accustomed to films that flash back and flash forward. Contemporary young-adult books like *The Perks of Being a Wallflower* and *Life of Pi* offer superb examples of cinematic writing. At the same time, short explosive passages have been present in autobiographical works for centuries—from the memoirs of Casanova and Benjamin Franklin, three hundred years ago, to those of Gabriel García Márquez and William Kennedy in this century.

I may not have been alone in my experimentation with autobiographical style, but I am certainly far afield from my business books.

In the end, I was convinced that the best way to reach those whose histories were least like my own was to approach the feast of my life wielding both the fork of facts and the spoon of fiction. Only through literature can we represent both facts and higher facts. Rudy agreed—and suddenly, my longing to share my life became a book.

For the world of personal narrative is about gain and loss, freedom and fate. But mostly it is about the power of memory—

an art form that is accessible to us all. It is through memory that we triumph over loss, and it is memory that renders the impossible probable—and the dead merely missing.

BP
Saratoga Springs, New York

Introduction

"I count myself in nothing else so happy
As in a soul remembering my good friends."
—WILLIAM SHAKESPEARE, *RICHARD II*

My name is Bruce Piasecki.

I know that's a long name, and an odd one. It has proven difficult for many Americans to pronounce and even to remember. Once, when I had rented a home situated high above the fog of Tennessee's Great Smoky Mountains, the landlord eyed me sideways, refusing to turn over the key until I had verified that I was, in fact, the strange fellow with the small family he was expecting. I pronounced and spelled my name slowly, making sure he heard. But when I got to the "a" and then the "s" followed by the "e" then the "c"—he interrupted with, "Wait a minute now, son! Letters can't fit together that way in Tennessee!" When I persisted, he handed over the keys, saying "Well, I suppose you speak pretty good American, for a Polack."

I start with my Polish name because I can still remember the out-of-body sensation of watching myself as my grandmother—my *Bapci*—tried to teach me to say it: "Pi-a-sec-ki, Pi-a-sec-ki." This was the beginning of my ability to see myself in the third person, which is how I have written my story. You can blame my name.

My Bapci, who spoke only Polish, held dominion over my early attention like an exotic queen. Her attempts to teach me to say my name that day persisted for nearly an hour. Later that same day, she and I played an amazing game of catch. Many years

1

afterward, my mother, Lillian, would say, "There is no way you could have played catch with Bapci, Bruce. She was already totally blind by then."

My mother may have insisted it wasn't possible, but I can still remember the wind swirling around my grandmother that day, the bandana in her hair, the Eastern European patterns on her blouse, her aged fingertips, and how proud she was that I could catch what she had thrown my way. And I *do* remember that catch, vividly—even as I prepare to turn sixty within a few short months. I also remember her catching the ball, many times. I remember the ball bouncing around near her breasts, and her arthritic fingers groping for it in this new world. And I remember her insisting that I pronounce my name the correct Polish way. That, I'm afraid, I never got right.

My grandmother died a few years later. Her death was not my first major loss: that would have been the death of my father, Walter, when I was three. There would be other losses to follow—not necessarily deaths, but endings or disappearances. This book traces my encounters—some real, some imagined—with the "missing persons" who have shaped my life.

During the past seventeen years, as I wrote *Missing Persons*, I came to see that telling stories about my life continued to actively shape my identity—the sense of who I was, and who I had been. I felt that the crucial relationship between memory and identity was best captured in a cinematic vision of personal history—complete with close-ups, tracking shots, flashbacks, and the occasional lurch of the handheld camera. I hope to have captured these moments, these magical memories, in a series of vignettes that are housed in the three parts of this book.

The vignettes that make up Part One explore what it felt like to grow up poor, to make it as a basketball player, and to find myself in the early 1970s on full scholarship at Cornell University. I was raised near the railroad tracks of West Islip, Long Island, by a widowed mother who took in foster children from a variety of racial and ethnic backgrounds. Even through high school, most of my teachers didn't believe that the Chinese or Puerto Rican kids they saw me hugging in the hallways during school or after basketball games were my brothers and sisters. My youth was magical, but leaving home and moving on to college was even more so. It was like manna from heaven—except that the manna was actually chocolate-coated bread and full of the nutrition (and poppy seeds) I had desperately needed on the courts and in the alleys of West Islip.

It was at Cornell that I met my magical wife, Varlissima. That is not her real name. I would like to have used her real name, but since my Sicilian-American wife is mostly American now—as well as being reserved, private, and far better educated than I— she insisted that I use a fictitious name in this book. Was this to ensure that her real name would remain unknown? Was it to protect the innocent? Was it her way of distancing herself from the facts and fantasy of my life? I think it was because of her deep humility, which renders memoirs fundamentally foreign to her way of being.

The vignettes in Part Two explore the delights and sensuality that come with a successful path in life, as well as the many fears we face as we age. For me, during the long valley of middle age, the magic of my life with Varlissima was complicated by the growth and success of my management consulting firm, which necessitated global travel; by the emergence of an increasingly strong desire to establish myself as a writer; by the death of my mother; and by the presence of the many muses in my life.

One of the central characters in this part of the book is Darlene—who actually exists and who has indeed improved the life of my family and my firm. But like other characters in the memoir, Darlene is a combination of herself and others I've met as I traveled the long road of middle age. How else to sum up that magic but through the composite flowers before you?

While echoing some of the themes found in Parts One and Two, Part Three is perhaps the most magical section of all. Inspired by a hopeful passage from best-selling author Oliver

Sacks about life after eighty, this part involves the fascinating idea that one's reputation can continue in the future. It presents a flash forward of my life—a visionary journey of memories and new adventures—during my final decades.

When I think back to my childhood memory of playing catch with my grandmother all those years ago, I can still hear my mother's voice telling me that it could not have happened. But the memory was absolutely real to me. In that same manner, the future vision of my life—the essence of Part Three—is as vivid and real as those moments with my beloved Bapci.

For once we come to appreciate the power of memory, we can make out the patterns that will likely precede our end. This might prove the most magical stage of all.

PART ONE

THE DISCOVERY OF COLETTE

"We have our secrets, and our needs to confess.
We may remember, in childhood,
adults were able to look right through us, and into us,
and what an accomplishment it was when we,
in fear and trembling, could tell our first lie."

—R.D. LAING
THE DIVIDED SELF

Prelude

Innocence and Youth

THE THING ABOUT LIFE IS THAT IT DOESN'T END, until it does. Corporate and personal crimes, however elaborate, end. Days with each muse, however wonderful, end. Jobs end, secrets end, even bad illnesses end. Loves end.

They all go missing.

Yet this life, in the end, is subsumed by youthful memory.

More massive than identity, memory makes our loves loveable or worthy of disdain. All goes onward in youth, and as Walt Whitman suggested, "nothing collapses, and to die is different than what anyone supposed, and luckier." Part of the art of living is learning how to live with the deeper art available to all: the art of good memories.

His father died young, but he continued on.

His early loves died, but he found a larger love.

His early business efforts, in the deepest sense, failed. But he continued onward and upward.

Memory organizes around the first lie, the first love, the first set of hopes and ambitions, and builds from them a magnificent mansion of missing persons. Memory filters and flatters, flattens then elevates. It does not boast; it is like a secret toast, celebrating life in all its foolishness and power.

After years of searching for novelty, after many wrong turns on the icy roads of relationships, he gained his greatest ground—

his traction in life—by creatively remembering his youth. This was the first bold step he took, the fortunate stumble that allowed forward motion.

To fight past the abrupt and paralyzing words of youth, to jump past the feelings of being isolated, crazed, confused, alone, terrified, wild, seeking—he began by retelling stories of a recalled youth, "a mythic Bruce," as his wife called it. Memory allows all this.

The setting for most of the Part One vignettes is Long Island, New York. These vignettes begin with his earliest memories at about age five and extend to when he was nearly forty. Because his meeting of Jay Parini, the noted writer, in the course of this part, involves a rapid return to his earlier self, some of the vignettes that end Part One start in Middlebury, Vermont, where Jay lives with his family.

This homage to his earlier self, a literary self, starts at Jay's place and continues with flashbacks to Long Island, Cornell University, and the beaches where he was born. In this way, Part One ends, in the deepest sense, with where this mythic Bruce first began—in the instructive trauma of his birth. And this full circle of Part One is then complete with the discovery of his daughter, Colette.

UNCLE ZIGMUND

LONG ISLAND, NY, 1960s

WHERE HIS FATHER HAD NEVER BEEN, his Uncle Ziggy walked. Even many years later, he could hear the click in that walk, Uncle Ziggy's swagger. Uncle Zigmund brought the Old World out of him, and the New World into him.

Standing strong and bronzed from his work as a Long Island landscaper, Uncle Ziggy had the build of a Polish Hercules. Zigmund was a funny man, a sportive man, a big friendly man. People smiled when near him. That was his gift to the New World.

"The people out there," he would say in his half-earnest, half-jovial Polish accent, "they give me a typed list of things to do—some sod here, some pines there, some new pruning here. They do not know what they really want! So I bury the list and do what *I* want. And they thank me. America is wonderful."

Members of Ziggy's extended family—from curious cousins to outraged adults—adopted this New World technique of defiantly ignoring the landowners. They, too, would rip up their lists, and proceed boldly.

"I had a toothache," he once said at Christmas dinner. "So I drank half a bottle of vodka—good vodka, the best—but the pain was still there. I got in my new car. I was on the Long Island Expressway before I knew it. Something in me said I'd better get off this wide highway, not to miss the turn to the dentist. So I did, and I swayed off the road a little, and took a nap near the turn. When I woke up, the tooth hurt even more, so I drank the other half of the bottle. When I got to the dentist's office—where I noticed that he could use some more of my shrubs—the receptionist asked me, "Do you have an appointment?"

Knitting together his thick eyebrows, Zigmund paused for the punch line. "Hey, you folks are a joke. You give me an appointment when I know no pain, and now that I am full of pain you cannot help me. I thought America was the land of opportunity. Where is the opportunity, Doc, to fix this damned tooth?"

Ziggy had a famous son who made it to Notre Dame on a football scholarship. Zigmund would call him collect in South Bend, Indiana: "Hello operator, good day to you Madame, this is Zigmund Yashevski calling Zigmund Yashevski. Please connect me now." Again and again, there would be a click at the other end—as the Lily Tomlin-like operator, imagining Uncle Ziggy to be no more than a prankster, hung up. Bruce thought about the oddness in Ziggy's insistence every time he found himself making that extra phone call for business. Zigmund was always there, egging him on to make that extra call even when they hung up.

Loud and colorful alarms went off in his young head, whenever he spent any time with Uncle Zigmund—the outspoken but victorious rebel of the family, the guy who thought he could make something of his life in this new America.

Ziggy was sportive yet dead serious, like a coastal Long Island storm. Ziggy had something about him that left a lasting impression—something classic, in an old New World way, and something disturbingly naked and honest.

EDWIN TORRES AND SUIE YING CHANG

LONG ISLAND, NY, AGE 7 to 17

EDWIN TORRES AND SUIE YING CHANG were his brother and sister, his Adam and Eve. While he had watched other foster brothers and sisters, from different races, from distant regions, come and go, Edwin and Suie stayed the longest in his memories.

While he had other people press near him now that he was a high school basketball star, it was the bounce and hope in Edwin's voice and Suie's dark round eyes that tracked his moods the most in youth. When they were sad, so was he. He felt that he was their protector, and the only one in his neighborhood thinking about where their next dollar might come from. He felt these foster brothers and sisters depended on him. He knew this in a primal way, in a way that was deeper than the prejudices that surrounded him.

After his father, Walter, died, the Veteran's and social security benefits were not adequate to feed and clothe the family. He saw that early in life. While his teachers and coaches chose to ignore such topics, he knew he would need to earn his way out of this predicament.

His mother could not afford a car. They never ate out. The only book of consequence in the house was the Bible. He started working at age ten—washing white walls on cars, working as a landscaper on Mongoon's Landing, laying sod like his Uncle Ziggy—to build that family purse. Lillian, his mom, left factory work and opened their home to foster children, which gave them a small but steady income. Locked into this arrangement, he felt close to his foster brothers and sisters most of the time. He remembers that fine day when he first received his working papers at the Rotunda of Beach Street. He was in his teens, and he felt at last ready to serve them.

Edwin was Puerto Rican and hyperkinetic—always rocking, always moving, always in trouble at school. "Edwin is a monster," a principal told him at Westbrook, many years before he had learned to fight back with words. The experts said Edwin was hyperkinetic because his biological parents were heroin addicts. Edwin was the only brother that stayed for more than six years, until he went missing. Most of the others were adopted by other families in a matter of months or a few years. He viewed this as a message. The accumulated worth of those losses defined his sense of what was missing in his life.

Suie Ying was born with birthmarks on her arms and legs, purplish maps that told the nuns at the New York City Catholic Foundling Home that she was a mix of Han Chinese and Samoan. Margaret Mead herself had once looked over her smallish body, and pronounced her "special and odd." There were other scars on Suie Ying's young body from a mother who had left her on a lit stove in Spanish Harlem. But that was before she found her real mother in Lillian.

His biological sister, Terry, was five years older than he, a saint-like Teresa, named after her patron saint. Never wronging any of the new foster kids, always praying for them, striving to be good before the peering eyes of God. Terry would marry her first high school sweetheart, Richard, and at times, go to Mass each and every afternoon when she left West Islip. His cousins Diane, Chris, and Steven were ever-present, warm, and caring family members, and neighbors during the reign of Suie and Edwin. His warm and likeable Cousin Steven affectionately referred to him as "cousin big head," noting how he leaned into a talk for emphasis. Chris died in his late forties; Diane moved south.

After his father died, his Uncle Steve, biological father of Chris, Diane, and Steven, was the father of both families in his attention and care. Good humor is what they all shared. There was a special bond that glued them together tightly, despite Walter's absence.

In contrast to his biological and foster siblings, he was an angry young man. By age fifteen, he had turned his athletic training into a weapon. This made him firmly capable of harming people on and off the court. He was a three-letter man during high school: a point guard on the basketball court, an aggressive center half on the soccer field, a shot putter and captain of the track team. All of these sports left scars—"knees of a hundred year old," his first surgeon noted; but he knew he had caused more harm to others than to himself. He called the scars "battle wounds," and wore them with some pride.

At home at 358 Oakwood Avenue, in that small house near the railroad tracks, his family lived. His grandmother, his *Bapci,* was going blind—so his mother and his wonderfully generous Aunt Ann cooked for at least a dozen of them on weekends. His Uncle Steve was never far off—always ready to give him a lift to a job. Uncle Steve's eyes were so bad they saved him from the draft, so he was always there—steady, kind, and loving.

Uncle Steve, a janitor at the local junior high, had a light-green van big enough to take the extended family all over Long Island—and to Mass at Our Lady of Lourdes Church in West Islip. Bruce came to love most of the Island that this van could reach, and he blissfully ignored the rest. Dix Hills and Northport and Oyster Bay were other worlds, the realm of royalty, and as far off from his imagination and longing as the moon before JFK.

The van lasted a good decade, from when he was age seven to seventeen. His cousin Steven was a superb mechanic, the technical guy amongst all those factory-bound kids. Steven would later convert this ability to fix things into a fine job as a United Nations engineer, wiring for security, wiring for microphones, and recording some of the most famous visitors of the century there.

He would hang up the pictures of Steven's travels next to the picture of the green van he kept on his fridge. As time passed, he was both frightened and ennobled by this green van that gave him his first glimpse of a larger world—a world that seemed too big to him at times.

Somehow this crowded, active absence allowed him to develop a feverish and a sportive view of his life. He learned to take heed of small immediate pleasures like a mother's meal—the crisp crusts of her apple pies—but he still knew what his distant, invisible father meant when he said that life was "one damned thing after another."

He ran everywhere, dribbling his basketball. Years later, he would find that Lillian had saved this worn basketball in her attic. She had said that for Christmas it was the only thing he wanted. He was an articulate jack-in-the-box, springing out most mornings in glee, a self-consuming clown with some spring and splatter in his ways. Beneath the box, the resentments of poverty sat still and angry, seldom stirring, except at game time.

He tried to capture the complex feelings of being at once thankful for his origins and driven from them. He wrote, even at age twelve, poems about what was sweet and what was sour in his life. He was everywhere and nowhere by now, a boy and a man, wanting and satisfied.

MARY BETH AND TRESPASS

NEAR MONTAUK HIGHWAY
WEST ISLIP, NY, 1970

THE EMPTY HOUSE, ABANDONED BUT NEAR, proved a perfect unexpected spot for teenage passion. Mary Beth had discovered it across Montauk Highway, not far from her St. John's Catholic High School, a brick sanctuary with plenty of cameras even then. He could still hear the cars rush by, racing for an advantaged position up the ramp to Robert Moses Bridge and his favorite white sand beach.

Her father made films in Manhattan. Her mother—lively, and interested in his early poetry—was on the West Islip Library Board. Like her mom, Mary Beth never used their massive home to lord over him. They met several times at her home, in the basement of this "never tell" Everdell Avenue mansion, with its yellow veneers and Italian velvet drapes. Her father played cards with author Mario Puzo in the dining room, she said, before Puzo became famous for writing *The Godfather* as well as the screenplay for the award-winning movie of the same name.

The afternoon that Mary Beth brought him to the abandoned house, he was in faded shorts and a T-shirt marked from landscaping. Mary Beth said she liked the smell of grass and turf, boy and man. He knew nothing else. And it was Mary Beth, so tiny, who encouraged this early trespass.

It felt fine to him as well, being able to be in town, yet so far from the sight of his world near the tracks. But he also felt it far too easy, far too natural. While his shorts slipped down, he realized in a long repetitive playback, it was not his, but rather Mary Beth's trespass. He would come to see that later. Back then, however, he fancied it his conquest.

The abandoned couch was in better shape than the one he occasionally slept on at home. Whenever his knee hurt too much to climb up the ladder (built by Walter) to his own bunk bed, which he shared with siblings, he would sleep on the couch in the living room.

That day, Mary Beth caressed the back of his right knee. She was intuitive, athletic, easing exactly the spot where the pain centered, where the tear slowed his basketball game. He was now ready to return to practice with Coach Smith. She wanted him to stay with her in the abandoned house until her dad returned home from work, perhaps so she would not be seen coming home from the wrong part of town. Mary Beth stood there in a strange light, demanding that he stay.

He picked up her colorful steel bangles from the purple sofa and placed them back on her thin but not fragile wrists. Mary Beth had the wrists of a tennis player and the thighs of a runner. Despite the strength of her request, despite the power in her stance, he noticed how her demands had no sway over him. She was to leave him the following week. Early the next year, she would find herself pregnant at sixteen. She claimed the father a wonderful legendary lacrosse player from town.

He moved on. The abandoned home remained for several decades before it fell. St. John's Catholic School, its icons still intact, continues to function by genuflection and need.

AN ANGRY YOUNG MAN

LEAGUE ONE BASKETBALL, LONG ISLAND, 1965 to 1972

WHEN HIS TEAM PLAYED against powerful opponents like Brentwood, a *Newsday* journalist wrote of him as "Chicken Little," saying he could bring down the sky with his long shot.

He could still recall most of the games he'd been in—major league or pickup—and most of the moves he had gotten away with. The bank shots that had swirled around and around and then dropped in meant everything to him. Anger may have urged a shot, but it was good fortune that allowed the swoosh. He was a shooter—and a performer—from day one on the courts.

Coach Smith spotted this ability to thrill, to absorb the limelight, early in him, in eighth grade—moving him up to varsity at age fourteen for four years in the spotlight. On the court, he turned his rage into winning baskets by driving the baseline, taking hits from the bigger players, and converting the third point in a free throw. He would not smile, they said, but just do it again. If an opponent figured that move would be likely again, he'd pull up rapidly with a soft sweet classic jumper.

In memory, he was mostly that angry young man.

The game of basketball transformed his focus. The stoic rage of his youth became acceptable to parents and lovers and teachers because of basketball. He jokingly referred to this as his "MVP license," not having a driver's license let alone a car. And he knew, deep down, he didn't even need to hit every important shot for them to remain pleased with him. The point was to take the risk for the town, to make the move, earn with spit and fire the crowd's respect and wonder. By his last high school playing season, he was worn and hurt, but there were thousands in his stands. When he shot his free throws, he never heard a word.

For the rest of his life, he cultivated the thrill of being a serious shooter during game time. Indeed, it was his willingness to shoot, to make the try with focus and zeal, that helped him move from being the kid of a factory worker to the kid on a scholarship at Cornell University.

The early death of his father, the life of poverty before college, the sweaty fear that he would never prove a writer of consequence—these things could have made him a bitter and nasty man, another petty man. Instead, in a magical transfiguration, somehow they made him what he was: persistently self-inventive. He was ready for game time in most situations. He developed endless ambition, which translated into a long willingness to practice and to give it a try.

ENCOUNTERS WITH AL OERTER AND MARCUS AURELIUS

EARLY READINGS AND AN EARLY ENCOUNTER ON COMPETITIVENESS, 1971

WHEN HE WAS OLDER, he read in the Science section of *The New York Times* about wondrous cognitive mapping techniques that made it possible to watch a patient's thought paths. The strange thing was that he felt, as early as the 1970s, that he could do the same on his own, with his own life—without a machine and without the tools of science. The early death of his father gave him this intuitive gift—this ability to perceive himself in the third person, to see himself assume the form of a shot both before and while it occurred. He could watch himself watch himself without tape, without machines.

This third-person gaming became habitual.

The habit grew from year to year, and it allowed him to stop short of the mirroring that had brought down Narcissus. Soon the gift became whimsical, sportive, a fun part of every day. It wasn't too serious; it was sportive seriousness.

During his twenties and thirties, he came to feel that he was watching thoughts, rather than actors and actresses, in all the greatest films he had ever seen. He could still remember his first Fellini film, and how it helped him realize that he had watched his entire life as if it had been a film; not in sequence, but in passion. Thought was not a game, it was *the* game. He had learned how to "perform while withdrawn." This phrase—from one of his early poems—stuck with him.

The strange, stern thug-like thought paths of Marcus Aurelius grooved his mind during those days off the court; Mr. Plumer, his best high school teacher, had given him his own paperback edition of the emperor's *Meditations*. Aurelius helped him get past the good-boy looks of his yearbook. He was now a bastard on the court, and now fierce in his mind. After reading Marcus Aurelius, he would be awakened by night sweats, by a froth stirred in his dreams. During the day, he'd catch himself thinking he could control Coach Smith during time-outs, twist the crowd when on the court, shape their thoughts to understand his game.

He was beginning to worry about the internal dialogue between himself and Marcus Aurelius. He then talked his way out of this worry through a chance exchange with the great athlete Al Oerter of Long Island.

Oerter was an Olympic champion in the discus throw. He was the first athlete to win a gold medal in the same individual event in four consecutive Olympics—a feat matched only by Carl Lewis in the long jump. Al was a large impressive athlete, who, after a serious injury, used the West Islip football field to practice his throws to increase his strength so he could continue to compete. Bruce would watch Al practice early some mornings before school, and then watch the shot putter return after his basketball practice at night.

Coach Smith introduced the athletes. Smith called Al "a natural thrower," someone who had already become the NCAA discus champion decades before practicing in West Islip. Al had grown up in New Hyde Park, so he knew about Long Island, and about its athletes. He asked the younger basketball player, "So what are you thinking when you hit those thirty free throws in a row?"

He answered, "Not much, Al. I cannot even hear the crowd."

Al said it was the same for him. Whether discus or shot put, he focused so hard he could not see or hear the crowd.

He took enough time away from his practice that day to recall that "persistence is the only real king for an athlete." Al spoke about how his career was almost over in 1957—when, at the age of twenty, he was nearly killed in a car accident. He had recovered in time to compete in the 1960 summer Olympics in Rome, where he was a slight favorite over his teammate, the world record holder Rink Babka.

The exotic nature of the European last name kept his attention. He asked, "So what happened, Al?"

"Well, Babka was leading for the first four of the six rounds, but persistence is the king. Babka paused to give me some advice before the fifth throw," and Al recalled, in a great elongated retrospect, "that pause, that friendly pause, I guess, was all the rest I needed that day." Al Oerter then threw his discus 194 feet and 2 inches, setting a new Olympic record.

In a later Olympics, Al Oerter was bothered by a neck injury, and then had torn cartilage in his ribs right before a key competition. But again, "persistence was the king of the day," Al recalled. It was a lesson Bruce had no trouble believing from then on. Al closed the talk with this advice: "If you need to call out to Marcus Aurelius to keep it all straight, then hell—go and call out the name Marcus, Bruce. It doesn't matter who you pray to during a competition, as long as you pray!"

WITH LEFTY AT THE UNIVERSITY OF MARYLAND

COLLEGE PARK, SUMMER OF 1972

NO ONE IN HIS RIGHT MIND CAN LIVE THE LIFE OF AURELIUS—so it was a joke for him to think that way into his youth! Especially for a factory kid in the wrong place at the wrong time. Somehow he got this joke about his life, and came to enjoy it.

He viewed this Aurelius mask he assumed like a joke. It was both a gift and a joke at the same time. Most did not get this joke yet of his life. But if Al Oerter got it, and if Mr. Plumer got it, to hell with everyone else, he thought that summer. Many felt him solemn and a bit too serious for his britches. He knew all this was merely a frame to look at the world and skip by orbiting harshness and its constant of ridicule. It became his way to sidestep past circumstance, and enjoy something new through a lens of discovery. He felt convinced that this gave him the sportive right to talk of himself in this third person.

This became a habitual form of self-reflection, even in his college applications. "Bruce will get the graham crackers after he gets the milk for his mom, and will then apply to Yale before Princeton," the Princeton application recorded, stating this a "practical way to size up his chances." He knew a serious candidate would not mention graham crackers in a college application, and he knew enough of his chances to be spoofing Princeton by mentioning first Yale.

He viewed it all as a joke at this point, and the sportiveness freed him to find who wanted him. Otherwise the world would have been far too large. Nonetheless, the authorities must have all thought him a lunatic! Even in high school, he acted the role of Marcus Aurelius in class—austere, articulate, and self-determining, on and off the court, controlling his crowds.

The first person must have died twice by the time he found Big Ben, once in reading Aurelius, then again in discovering and then intensively reading Benjamin Franklin. He didn't care who the second person was, actually, when asked. Seven hundred free throws in practice each day, dribbling for three hours daily, four on weekends, sprints, driving with both hands. There were some early results from this Aurelian twist of thought—and it bred new forms of hope to play basketball in larger leagues.

This all peaked for him during a summer scholarship in 1972, a full ride with meals and clothes, to the Lefty Driesell Basketball Camp at the University of Maryland. The gym was huge, the meals were remarkable, his teammates were fundamentally faster and better than any he had ever played with. Lefty Dreisell, by now a legendary coach at UMD, gave him on the side extra cash, meals, and a bigger head for sweeping the floor when others left for rest. Perhaps his cousin Steven was right: He was becoming "Cousin Big Head." His wingspan kept growing as well; soon his shoulders resembled those of Uncle Ziggy and those of his cousin Zigmund, who played football for Notre Dame.

He said to himself each late afternoon that summer, "But Bruce could use an even bigger body," as he swept. He felt often that his head was too heavy for the rest of his body, so he kept lifting more and more weights to reshape his upper torso. His legs had already been shaped from the miles of cutting lawns, from when he was ten to the end of high school. He felt all this running the best way for him to appreciate his born limits. He'd run ten to twenty miles a day to find better and better pick-up games, some in Babylon, some in Bay Shore, and the best in Brentwood.

He liked sweeping for the coach's cash at the University of Maryland's big-time floor. He was proud pushing that broom. Lefty's brooms were always like brand new, so much fresher than the worn and warped broom he grew up with in West Islip. Lillian's sole broom had been worn into a tilt.

In College Park, at age seventeen, he walked with the legends of the game. Already over 225 pounds of upper arm and leg muscle, at six feet one inch, he hung out each day with Mitch Kupchak, at six feet eleven inches. Mitch was a natural center. Bruce was not a natural star—some thought of Bruce as a six-foot, 228-pound point guard who could shoot "unnatural." Point guards are supposed to be lean, swift, and severe. He was neither lean nor swift, but many found him coachable. Mitch would star in college, get hurt early as a pro, and then by the new century become General Manager of the Los Angeles Lakers. Mitch was not the only UMD camper that summer who would turn pro.

Guarding as best he could Earl "the Pearl" Monroe for a week of camp, running near Kevin Laugherty of the Baltimore Bullets— and a few times, scoring over Kevin but not Earl—those were the days of wonder. He hung with many college-bound future pros, like Kenny Henry, realizing they were destined for jail, or the street, or the biggest leagues. Kenny could dunk from a standstill, effortlessly. Some of Kenny's behavior, like wearing a dog chain around his neck, frightened Coach Lefty. So Lefty asked Bruce to "reason with Kenny if he wants to be with you on the all-star pick-up game next week."

Never good at patience or skilled in impulse control, Kenny Henry removed the dog chain with his naked hands at mid court, and kept running, throwing the chain at the coach on the bench. Kenny starred that week in the all-star game, but wound up in jail before the end of the next year, never making it to college.

Keeping his distance each day, he now became aware of how limited his body potential actually was. He began to ask Marcus: Could any of this innate anger and competitiveness be translated into a life outside the court?

It was now late summer after the University of Maryland, and a few days before his entry to undergraduate school. From his reading of Marcus Aurelius, he found another thought path come to him late one Saturday night when Edwin was taunting Suie downstairs. He had several basketball-based scholarship offers to entertain that week. (He would much later find out that Lillian had kept each college offer in a metal box beneath her clothes, along with notes and letters from her long-deceased husband.)

His right knee was in constant pain, his left having its first cartilage tear that season. He had never contemplated college before, so he was hyper alert in his chair. His sister Terry, their grandmother, and his mother were preoccupied with their favorite TV comedy show. Suie and Edwin paused in their shenanigans.

The laughter from downstairs lingered as he thought about his near future. He paused another ten minutes upstairs alone to recall the beauty marks on Mary Beth's sun-tanned shoulders from the day before, and her long athletic thighs. She was everything to him that day. Even today, he cannot picture the face of Mary Beth's movie-producing father, but he can see the shape of that shoulder. He would resist going downstairs with his family until he completed the mission, until he controlled the thought.

Then he got it: unlike those who consume themselves in immediacy, he could balance his lust with the thoughts of Aurelius. He then thought long and hard about Sally, then about Mary Beth, then again about the muscular leanness in Sally's thighs, before he approached either of them in school. He often stood near them in silence, provoking them to speak first as a stupid test of his manhood and his needs.

This ability to see himself in the third person gave him a choice to resist immediacy: he could choose Sally or Mary Beth, succeed in this college or that one. He was playing another kind of game.

HURRICANE SANDY

LINDEN AVENUE, ITHACA, NY

BACK IN 1976, HE WAS AN UNDERGRADUATE on full scholarship at Cornell. She was an alluring grad student, with time to skip over to his place on Linden Avenue, one of the run-down student sections of the college town.

Sandy seemed to have come from a different part of the world, an Elizabethan place of sparkle and hope, and this he found an early example of plentitude. He found it a worthy game to test his heart and his words. "Speak low," she noted, "if you speak love."

They shared the attention of M.H. Abrams, one of Cornell's most distinguished professors of literary history. She would stay after class as much to hang with the new boy in class as with Professor Abrams. That pipe-in-hand legend of literary history taught them much.

She was of Russian descent, sweet as summer could find, and he was purebred Polish. He thought of himself as Polish. They were attracted to each other. Some days, she would wiggle his big toe after the mid-afternoon Ithaca storms, and, eye to eye, they would talk of literature, line by line. He found that he could use language to draw her near—and in touching her with words, he would lighten and strengthen their mortal and magical bond for life.

One bright day in May, looking like an angel, she asked, "Do you remember that classic Polish story *Bapci's Angel,* where the young boy's toe begins to wiggle in the hospital after his little brother prays exactly as his grandmother told him to? The motif works, doesn't it, Bruce, for both of us?" After a nod, they would melt into a sameness that only youthful sex allows.

Part One

It wasn't inspiration. It was better. He felt fluid, and the phrases kept erupting, on a good Ithaca day.

Each day with Sandy was like a Long Island hurricane, but in Ithaca. This was 1976, and he was now twenty-one, a man in bloom. It was pure passion, with little restraint. The numbers seventy-six and twenty-one seem magical even today, when he crosses them.

Back then, he still talked like a crewman. His brethren were certain his thick Long Island accent would fade away; and he himself believed that someday soon the elites of the school would wash out his mouth properly of all accent.

She was as beautiful as shooting stardust in the storybooks of old Russia. They shared a love of painted Easter eggs, and sweet Greek breakfasts downtown.

He had at about this time his first original thought: *I can have more—more of this storm, more from this soft warmth in Sandy's hands, this perpetual feeling from sex and talk after sex—and perhaps way more from literature than I was first told I could.*

Somehow, through Sandy, study had assumed increasing power. Over time, he built a worldview from his early longing for Sandy. "Hell," he thought, "if I can earn the attention of someone like Sandy, maybe it is all worth the time and trouble?" He imagined reading thousands of classics.

The gloom of his birth began to lift when he thought of her. Without knowing it, she helped him stay in Ithaca a full ten years, liberating his lifelong love of words and books. Even up there in icy Ithaca, he could still feel the wind from Long Island. His past, the ice, Sandy—they all mixed his memories into a frenzy of uncontrollable ambition and anger. After the storms, he knew that life could be so much more than where he first belonged.

She was a hurricane.

She was his coach.

He was beyond being Polish.

He had come alive.

THE BLIND ALLEY OF BIRTH

OAKWOOD AVENUE, WEST ISLIP, LONG ISLAND TO ITHACA, NY

RETURNING HOME ONE MID-TERM, he was amazed to realize that often his muses lingered as he moved from scene to scene; they traveled wherever he traveled.

Even when he was in the arms of Sandy, for example, he was not freed of his mother's watch. Lillian was limitless, like a London or a Manhattan. He could always hear the voice of one woman he knew within the voice of another woman he had just found; for they formed a rich composite in his mind, and they formed a large symphony in his soul.

The blind alley of his birth was an efficient way to describe the immediacy of the memories that haunted him.

His blind alley was the area surrounding his first home on Oakwood Avenue. He could wander anywhere, but he was still walking Oakwood Avenue, a blind alley that defined him far fuller than his decade of women at Cornell ever could. These memories were fantasies formed from facts, early forms of a life-long love. And taming the beasts within him was always about the geography of his first home.

Here was the paradox of youth in a nutshell. He did not choose his mother. Yet his mother shaped him. He lent Lillian money in time, and she said, "You owe me your life!" or "Get the mop!" He realized in retrospect that it was profoundly stupid to expect any cash repayment from his mother. She was the pond, the winter, and the thaw. She was his mother, and that was everything.

Throughout his youth he had run along this blind alley, grooved from the start—accepting the sweet gestures of Sandy as if they were distractions from the known, thrown as he was into this lovely game of life. And then suddenly, his mother helped him look up. His mother made him restlessly look up, like a prompt frog at dawn that escapes the descent of the first storm, and makes its special escape to the next pond. She helped him get that freeze out of his eyes.

Under Lillian's vigilant and watchful eyes, he finished his dissertation on "Walt Whitman and the American Estimate of Nature" despite barely considering college during his high school years.

In comparison to Lillian, everything else seemed seasonal.

LILLIAN ANN PIASECKI

ITHACA, NY, 1978

EVENINGS WERE REFLECTIVE. One February day, about a year after his discovery of Sandy, while now a new graduate student at Cornell, he imagined his mother aged, and near death.

He knew this to be perverse. But he also knew it to be necessary.

He was still a young man, no more than twenty-two, and she was still an active woman in her fifties, living alone on Long Island, with full control of her faculties. But during this particular visit she made to him in Ithaca, he chose to imagine her near death. It was part of the perversity in his third-person view; everything must be seen from a distance. He must be prepared for anything. He had watched the early death of his father, so why not witness the loss of his mother?

It was during that visit, that stark February week, when his boots were etched with ice, that she showed him how to construct a response to this jack-in-the-box life. She knew that he was getting lost in his memories, that he was taxed by his past. With humor and some remorse, she suggested that he outsmart his current options in order to face the work world. He had to learn how to father himself sooner rather than later. "Why not come back with me to factory life?" she asked.

This broke the freeze.

Nothing should be taken for granted when a mother tells a tale of a return to harsh origins like that. She was telling him to see past Cornell, see past the certain professorships, into what he must become—or else return, forever.

Before success, even before aspirations, Lillian's stories showed him a sweet, ripe, pear-like middle way.

Before the declarations in Christ,

Before the conversations of Socrates,

Before the resolve of a Marcus Aurelius,

She kept him clothed. She kept him young, despite the rigid demeanor and repressions inherent of graduate training.

She called them "elaborations," these stories he would share, stark "embellishments." When home, or over the phone, she told him these stories nearly every afternoon. When faced with something complex, he would always ask himself, "Well, what choice would Lillian offer?" Her tales were more basic, more fundamental than those that tied themselves onto every word of Christ or Socrates or Aurelius. It wasn't an exact script she had offered him. It was a mother's path for him to grow past his father.

A SECOND MOTHER

OUR PURPOSE IN LIFE IS A MYSTERY. His primary mother, the mother he saw every day of his youth, taught him to be alert and tender in the face of this mystery. Yet there was also another astonishing Lillian; tough, persistent, driven Lillian. He called this Lillian his "second mother."

Without a father, he felt he was entitled to celebrate a "second mother." Throughout his life, he found himself expecting women to have more than themselves in themselves, maybe because of their ability to bring life into the world. In looking at the deep strengths of his mother, he came to expect women to be volcanic, with a creative doubleness that brought the mystery of a man closer to himself—like when an artist first finds his most significant muse. This mystery in women also added to his sense of their valor.

When he left his first mother Lillian at her home on Oakwood Avenue to explore Cornell, this second mother got closer to him. This second, more authoritative mother grew in him each year as he physically grew more distant from West Islip. She taught him to accept his place by not stopping, to embrace the mystery that led to his calling by roaming a larger world. She taught him an openness that knew his place but wanted more.

She was a woman of spirit, and did not want material matters to weigh them down. Storytelling was their salvation. He was a man born to be a roamer, someone who had to test her principles against his larger world, again and again.

After a while, he concluded that this toughness, this persistence in Lillian, was something all women have within, but that these muse-like qualities are easier to access when the woman is free from a living husband. This belief in the power within single women resonated with his experiences with many basketball stars, whose moms raised the big boys themselves. Later, in business, he found this pattern often visible in the fiercest start-up enterprisers. It was not a consistent requirement for small business success, but he saw this often, this birth of the bold.

By the time he was in graduate school, he had come to believe that single mothers should be offered space in the Poets' Corner in Westminster Abbey, near the sharp nose and face mask of William Blake. But they are not even invited to the abbey. Instead, they walk home, with greasy hands from making millions of fasteners at the Dzus factory near the Long Island Railroad tracks, where he began.

So he would figure out other ways to celebrate the greatness in his second mom. Often the attempts proved futile, as if the act of her greatness was enough. There was something about this second mom that was invisible to others—something that only he could see.

He remembered his first trip back from Europe on scholarship, while he was a young Clarkson professor. He had saved his per diem to buy his mother an Austrian trail coat: bright blue, with red trim, and the traditional emblem blazing.

She never wore it.

Decades later, he was helping her move some things out of her closet, and he asked why she had never worn the coat.

She said, "I would always rather be with you as I am, than become some made-up person I am not."

STORIES BY LILLIAN THAT LAST

THE LONG ISLAND RAILROAD TO
NEW YORK'S CATHOLIC FOUNDLING HOME

THREE STORIES capture the grace, the force, and the fascination of Lillian. Each provided lasting lessons. He remembers receiving two of those lessons as a young boy, during train rides back from Manhattan after visits to the Catholic Foundling Home. The third came decades later.

The first: "Bruce, when you meet guys like those you compete against on the basketball court or in business—just treat them with love. They will eventually do you and your family a lot of good."

She taught him so much about life, and about the control of anger. She taught him the difference between hanging his life up to dry in hollow expectations, and finding the right fit for his coat, and moving on.

The second: Another time, returning from a visit to the foundling home, he and his mother encountered a large rude beast who spoke to Lillian in an ugly way about the multi-racial kids who were "taking up space" on the train. "Bruce, leave a guy like that alone, for in two or three years he will explode on his own."

He might have been ten at the time, and large enough to take a good swing at the man. Instead, she taught him how to do so much more with less, how to benefit from emotions rather than swim in them forever. They let the rude beast sit alone.

The third: One sunny June day at his home across the street from the Old Stone Church, his mother surprised him again, deeply. She was in her early eighties at this point, he in his early fifties.

The day was quiet, with few birds, and the pond was almost silent. He and his mother were sitting in the backyard after he had returned from doing some international traveling for work. To rest, he was reading to her the *New York Times* extended obituary on the life and work of Erik Erickson.

As he was explaining the difference between Erickson's view of multiple journeys in life and the Freudian presumption of one big identity crisis, she said, "I have had six identity crises in my life." He paused in astonishment. Not a single cloud interrupted what came next.

"First when your father died, then when your sister left to get married, and then again when you left for Cornell." What came after that, he hardly had to ask. "I felt what Erickson means when my brother moved out to Albuquerque, when your Uncle Ziggy died, and then when I began to lose my mobility."

She knew that he had read the works of Sigmund Freud, whom she hated. That afternoon, she aligned her stars with Erickson. "Do not forget, Bruce, you wrote your dissertation about Walt Whitman because the father you never knew was called Walt."

A FUNERAL MESSAGE

OUR LADY OF LOURDES CHURCH,
WEST ISLIP, NY, 2009

LILLIAN LOVED THIS LONG ISLAND CHURCH—as much as she loved the sounds and smells of her home in West Islip.

The simple joys of her life were her saints, her meals, and her pleasantly unique conversations. She was like Walt Whitman all over again when at the Robert Moses beach—all happy and clear, most days. And like Walt, she saw meaning in death.

During the funeral ceremony, his sister Terry wrote heartfelt comments that by chance echoed Caedmon, without knowing it. She read: "Now let us praise the Guardian of the Kingdom of Heaven, the might of the Creator and the thought of His mind, the work of the glorious Father, how He, the eternal Lord, established the beginning of every wonder."

When Terry spoke, he felt the "He" she was referring to was Lillian, their culturally ignored but great mother. As an athlete, he knew there was something deviant in thinking the heavenly feminine, yet he also felt that she hovered over her family like a heavenly body. Without stern punishment, without much education, she had ensured that her children would remain under moral rule, and learn how to tame both the beasts around them and the beasts ticking in their hearts. Lillian did all this with little direct power and few resources. During her funeral, this growing awareness overwhelmed him. "What force granted her so much grace?" he began to ask—a discussion he carried with him for some time.

Since Lillian's death, whenever he visited Westminster Abbey and sat thinking of her, he felt best beneath the memorial to Oliver

Goldsmith. The back door to this often-ignored part of the abbey leads to St. Faith's Chapel, a hideaway chapel far from the throngs of people peering in at the popular entrance. And it was there, in this small chapel, after all these centuries of war, and under the words of the Oliver Goldsmith memorial, that he could sit in private prayer—without God, without dogma, simply with the sound and strong memories of his mother.

His mind goes there whenever he thinks of his mother. She is there, somewhere in the abbey. She is there—everywhere—in literature. She is always there, his Missing Person.

COASTAL BLISS

MEETING VARLISSIMA IN ITHACA
EARLY 1980s

HE THANKED GOD FOR SEASHELLS. When feeling generous, he even thanked the Long Island beaches where shells were found—free, adorable, and awaiting his hands. But he came to thank his wife even more.

Since his childhood, he had found great relief in looking through the Golden Nature guide *Seashells of the World*. Years later and far from the sea, he still had that $1.25 edition in his home office. He cherished this small book, and would page through it each time he was home on vacation from school. While Lillian often tidied up by throwing away all of his papers while he was away, she kept that book for his return, and sometimes stood it near her Bible.

Yet his most amazing find, his shell of shells, was his wife, Varlissima: a woman who contained all women. In the course of his life, he would come to believe there was something special and historic in a composite. Varlissima herself embodied these higher facts of a composite more clearly than he had ever seen in any shell. If there was any lasting meaning in the word "supernatural," it had to do with these formations of composites in his life, starting with Varlissima. She was part his mother, part his early lovers, yet completely herself.

Varlissima was at times as dark as the olive shells of Africa; at other times, she was white, with the shape and spin of a tulip shell.

Variety was the essence of Varlissima, a most passionate woman. Shakespeare could write about his dark lady and about his fair youth, but he would write about Varlissima, the woman who knew the oceans would rise years before the warning became real.

Her hand gestures, her raised eyebrows, her changeable smile proved alarming and more worthy than the simple shells of his youth. The heart and soul of Varlissima, this bright vegetarian from Yonkers, was pure energy to this ex-athlete. And the tension in being near her was always tender and alert.

During the 1980s, their first decade together, Varlissima would warn him that men can make beautiful things only in times of war. The entire history of Sicily proved that much, she said. But he felt, deep in his heart, that she was forgetting the bliss of coasts. "You have to fall in love with the process of becoming greater," she once whispered in his ear, with a whisper he had heard before only in shells.

His coaches had said the same thing about basketball, but Varlissima was saying it about their life.

She was capable of saying something profound after a set of disarming jokes. Some do this because they are shallow; she did it intimately. "Why were men given larger brains than dogs?" she once asked him at Sapsucker Woods outside the Cornell campus. "So they will not hump a woman's legs during the start of a cocktail party!" "Why does it take one million sperm to fertilize a female egg?" "Sperm refuse to stop and ask directions."

For years, he would walk with Varlissima—miles at a time, sometimes a dozen in a day—trying to calm her, hoping for calm in her. He wanted to hear that whisper again, the oceans within her. It often proved difficult.

In his memory, she remained troubled, as if in storm. This was part of her appeal, something only sex seemed to calm for the few first decades. Varlissima was the rage of Italian oceans, the chill outside each Roman *pensione* they strove to share.

Thirty years later, she still remembered how cold she had been the night she walked with him and a few friends to Midnight Mass on Christmas Eve in Venice. In her he sensed the inevitability of flooding in San Marco, and the waist-deep changes during their days together. She was oceanic and rising before him each day. "What did the African elephant say to the naked American businessman?" "How do you breathe through something that small?"

He never really suspected the consequences of sea rise until he met Varlissima. "Here are a few things no man in my life will ever say: 'Sometimes I just want to be held.' 'Fuck the NBA finals, let's go shopping tonight!' 'Sure, I really love wearing those condoms.'"

She remained a shell of shells, full of variety, full of the charm of surprise, and the force of a storm. Between them remained a space, a difference of immense consequence and certain closeness.

WALKING WITH VARLISSIMA

EARLY TRAVELS, TRIPS TO SICILY
1981 to 2007

THE MASSIVE CHANK SHELL, with its smooth, glasslike curve, is found in a few parts of the world, mostly Ceylon and India. But, like the best of anything, it is traded widely. He had one on his desk when he first met his future wife. Nervously, as he was eyeing her shape, her smile, sensing his longing, and hers, he would look to the chank shell on that desk, to relieve some tension.

He had heard that in India, chank shells are collected by ambitious women, who cut them into ornamental rings and bangles. From the start, he felt Varlissima's ambition and she felt his. Sometimes left-handed chank shells—genetic defects—can be found on Hindu altars, mounted in gold. He felt the same way about Varlissima: she was a rare one indeed. The slant of light in the afternoon mounted her in gold. He would become a writer, and a businessman of some impact, if he could have her with him as he grew.

Yet they still had massive differences, differences larger than the seas between Sicily and the rest of Italia, full of sirens and myths, rich with fog and swift currents.

There must be a happier middle ground, he thought, between the strength of her seas and the wants of his loins, between the smart poverty of her thoughts and his taking off her pants. This was his internal argument for decades, being half a centaur, and half a very practical businessman. It was the tension between them that was supreme—but, unlike most supreme things, this tension lasted decades.

When frustrated, she would say: "What do men and floors have in common?" "If you lay them properly, you can walk on them for the rest of your life!" "What's the fastest way to a man's heart, if you are vegetarian?" (as Varlissima was). "A sharp knife through the chest." "What do Cornell men and pantyhose have in common? They either run, cling, or don't fit properly in the crotch."

"Keep your powder dry, Bruce," she once suggested in a sticky situation, "preserve it for our future use, so that when you need it, you can make magic for us." She was Sicilian for sure: intense, emotional, relentless, superstitious. It would take years before he could afford to bring them to Sicily, but when he did, opening that golden door made remarkable sense.

Sicily's seaside resort of Taormina was built on Mount Tauro in the fourth century before Christ, by exiles from the nearby Greek colony of Naxos, who merged happily with the local populations. This was clearly a part of their genius, this easy merging with folks quite opposite. The town first became famous in the 1700s, when rich young Europeans included it in their grand tour after college. By the time he and Varlissima arrived at Taormina, it was a tourist destination with international sparkle and intrigue. So walking up the steps to the theater of Taormina with Varlissima fit properly, in a primal archeological way. Whenever he was depressed about her stubbornness, he'd recall each of the many worn stone steps leading up to the theater, where the sound was supreme, and the view closer to heaven than anything he had ever seen.

The birds were hers, and the shorelines, and the steep rock steps. She was the world of Sicily by his side, and he loved that very much.

Life is always more important than work, she made him see at last—everything about her suggested that. "What do men and beer bottles have in common?" "They're both empty from the neck up!" "What do men and snowstorms have in common?" "You don't really know when they are coming, how long they'll stay, or how many inches you'll get till it's over!"

The Greek Theatre of Segesta in Sicily's province of Trapani is a perfect semicircle. This space offered them a generous panorama, exactly as dictated by the rules of ancient design.

As they walked along the beach, Varlissima would enrich the hike with intriguing idioms from around the world. "Did you know that when you are very angry—like I see you sometimes, Bruce, but rarely—the Chinese say that 'smoke belches from the seven openings on your head'?" She had a book of these idioms in her brain; he felt he could spot these special phrasings like tiny birds swirling around her red head, hidden in the thick of her hair.

Remembering their time at the Temple della Concordia, where one of the best-preserved temples of Greek antiquity in Sicily sits, he recalled that the temple had been converted into a Christian church in the sixth century. That is what, ironically, had safeguarded it from the normal neglect and destruction. Knowing this history, he figured out ways to keep Varlissima from the known harms and wrongs of time.

Like Lillian, Varlissima had her own magical way of refocusing his native competitiveness to make it less warlike when at home. She was educating him, making him ready for the ultimate gift of fathering Colette.

Varlissima had a variety of ways to stir those pots and imperfections within him. "Why do so many women fake orgasm?" "Because so many men fake foreplay." He found it best to listen, contemplate the sassy suggestion, and then climb on her again after the walk, whenever he found something warm and accepting in her. He always felt cleaner after a good go-round with her. "What is the difference between men and government bonds? Government bonds mature."

The hilarious underbelly beneath all their outward anger was inward love. It was their great differences and close intimacy that helped him sidestep self-destruction. They both shared a youth of poverty and books, a time of severe and liberating discoveries at Cornell, and many sweet evenings together. That was enough to keep them near each other for life.

One Sunday morning in Potsdam, where they had landed their first after-college jobs at Clarkson University, in the dead center of St. Lawrence County, she had given him two black eyes. It happened when she lifted her knees as he gingerly bounced back to bed on a very frigid North Country morning. The sound of his eyes quashing was something he never forgot. She left town the next day for a week of work elsewhere—a rare happening during those North Country days—so he had to quickly make up a story about his black eyes to protect his pride before seeing his students and his fellow ball players at the Clarkson gym. He claimed that the black eyes had resulted when a vindictive ballplayer responded to his head fake with double elbows.

Nothing was important enough for him to leave Varlissima— the incredible finely scripted letters he would find everywhere when he woke early, her meticulous kitchen notes about how she'd end the relationship if he left another coffee grind near her breakfast. He was in a double bind, and he came to like it. He wrote her extended letters of refutation during his travels but would not send them, mostly because he came to see them as stupid when he returned home.

For him, it was all about the coasts, and for her, it was all about the oceans. He suspected that it was this balancing calm that had attracted the volatile and ever-electric Varlissima to him in the first place—her eyebrows expressing urgent need, her legs jumpy to move or to be pinned down again. She once slipped in a warning to a new swimming mate: "If you really want a committed man, pick the best-dressed one in the mental hospital."

She coached him hard. "How do you find a blind man in a nudist colony? It ain't hard."

A MADDENING COUPLE

LEAVING POTSDAM FOR CASTLETON-ON-HUDSON, ROUND LAKE, AND SARATOGA SPRINGS
1990 to 1996

THEY MADE A MADDENING COUPLE to friends, who claimed they embodied opposites. She was the meat in the shell, and he was the shell. He was the aggressor, and she was one of the infinite who absorbed his aggression. She was becoming him, and he was becoming her. He could live with this tension; Mr. and Mrs. Tolstoy had. In fact, he used his sense of couple-hood to hide some personal and spiritual crises, and that felt good. She was the ocean, and he remained coastal in his bliss.

As they walked the long, skeletal coasts of southwest Sicily, they paused, hand in hand, to view the majestic waves, to feel the heat, and to breathe in the salty air. It was only the two of them there—before the discovery of Colette—and it was there that they never resolved their differences, and it was there that they became resolved.

One walks the earth alone or with a keen other. He found his keen other in Varlissima. Yet still she remained troubled, a woman stirred like a top of ceaseless emotion. He could eat a steak or take a long nap, and awake to find her looking lovely—and exactly like her volatile self, reading, but not calm.

The more she talked, the more her hair made sense to him. It was large hair, and red. Her soft voice made many youthful narratives in his mind. He wanted, so badly, to capture the essence of that voice to share it whenever he could. Otherwise, he feared it might disperse, like the misty memories of his father. After many decades with this wife, he started to write about their youth, and about his immense longing during their days with their daughter.

Together they began to recall the many missing persons who had visited their home. Writing their recollections was his way of honoring those who were gone. Unexpectedly, it also enabled him to become even more appreciative of the valor in women.

PREGNANT AND UNCHANGING

SARATOGA SPRINGS, NY
AUGUST 29, 1996

BY THE AGE OF FORTY-TWO, he knew he could no longer contain a woman like Varlissima. "Strong women contain too much flooding," he thought. The only way he and Varlissima could survive the flooding was to become more than a couple; for him, this meant becoming more than an academic, and embracing a life of action.

Embracing the threats of fanatics from long ago, the past failures of men with their women, and the certainty that things can go easily wrong in business—and will—Varlissima told him that the seas would rise up against his coasts, and that someday all men would perish from this earth. And with that she said, "Yes! Yes!" she would marry him.

The marriage took place in Saratoga Springs on Broadway at Café Panini restaurant. To perform the ceremony, they employed a Unitarian female minister, something not easy to find so near the six million acres of the Adirondack mountains. They were in their home, first built in 1770, a month before the marriage. This was a fine home that had once been burnt down during the French and Indian Wars, but its calming features and its large open expanse were exactly right for them.

Even when pregnant, Varlissima was amazing—walking, cooking, talking, being Varlissima. Some women are paused by the size and weight of childbearing. Varlissima found it liberating.

He saw that he and Varlissima could not, should not, stop walking as a couple; for if they did, they might forfeit their confidence, and never again regain respect for each other. They took long walks up to the hour before Colette was born on August 29,

1996. From that moment on, he knew that he would need to learn to appreciate Varlissima for what she was. That was a big part of coastal bliss.

The more she talked, the more he came to understand her hair. With the birth of Colette he was now ready to leave teaching. He had always felt a stranger in the paradise of the university. That was why he had established his own consulting firm in 1981, the year Cornell granted him his doctoral degree. It was to create an alternative to his dependence on anyone, even school life. Even back then, he had a sense of something more, something more actionable, more self-determining for his life. In short, it was his fear of having a boss that drove him to create something out of the blue.

He had had a motto from day one, from the first classes he taught during his PhD work at Cornell, where he noted that "actors speak of imaginary things as if they are real, but academics speak of real things as if they are imaginary." In fact, he had once made a mock business card with this motto on the back, the same day he had a Vietnam vet design his original company logo. Half sportive, half dead-serious, he had a life-long quarrel with his love of teaching. He could understand these paradoxes in himself now, for what made him different was exactly parallel to what made his Sicilian wife have red hair—it was for some higher reason.

With the birth of Colette, he would now need to position his newly formed consulting firm for success, not just for fun and for discoveries on what makes a business tick or a business fail. So while still an academic, teaching at Rensselaer's Lally School of Management and Technology, for the first few years of her life, he was earning double—from teaching and from consulting through his company. Then Toyota gave him a three-year offer that was so good he could not refuse, and he left all those years of teaching, with a smile to match his motto.

FRIDA AND HIS FLY

FANTASY WHILE TEACHING AT RENSSELAER, 1990 to 1996

WHEN HE FIRST MET FRIDA, he was glad that she had been dead for nearly sixty years. Otherwise, he might have needed to divorce Varlissima. He had met Frida in an art book. Frida was fabulous because he could not have her.

He was aware that he couldn't technically call her a lover, any more than his friends could call his cigar smoking safe. It was a boyish lie even to call Frida a friend, but it felt good to do so. Self-deception is an element of creation, he believed. That's what he found so pleasant and juicy about good art and good books.

There was a magical certainty in her eyes. In the end, he found that like all great art, she was only wiggling his wants all along, at no real risk to his family. There was a strange torture to her joined eyebrows that pleased him. His tightening pants remained a subject of distraction with her. Frida and his fly seemed connected at the level of his best neurotransmitters, like the words "Madonna" and "Milano" or "Frida" and "fly."

Her paintings made him twiddle with his fly. It did not matter what her husband, Diego, thought. It did not matter that he refused to visit her in Mexico City. She was immense, and immediate, and Frida. Over time, the world would come to see how much she mattered—and for her, that was all that mattered.

She became like a colorful orchid in his mind, wet and open and inviting. Her talk in Spanish made him want to hold her delicate neck, fondle her in English, and bring her head near. Her expressions said "Get closer," after all. He would not be able to resist, even as he aged. Her work would chronically disturb him, as all great art is meant to do.

That was why he was glad he never came across her work in any American museums until he was already committed. And while there was plenty of art in his offices, he never had a piece of Frida's art near. That would be like populating work with pornography, or eating dessert first.

He felt it wise to talk about her as a composite of all his past lovers—mostly to himself, but also to a few dear neighbors and friends who looked at him with longing in their eyes. They knew Varlissima was his answer long before he did.

ANOTHER VISIONARY

VARLISSIMA ON
A RARE CAMPUS VISIT, 1990

WHEN VARLISSIMA DRESSED LIKE THAT, the Holy Spirit would rise within him and clap, making him pay attention again and again. "Look at that torn kneecap in her jeans, the fine spikes that shape her jumpy legs, the lasting wars in her Sicilian eyes, the turbulent sea of her superb words."

College, graduate school, Potsdam, Albany, Castleton, Saratoga Springs, Ballston Spa, overseas: her slim blue jeans came along for all of this.

He was at ease with her, mostly after the excitement—a spent soldier, Nathaniel's marble faun. He watches her bend over to pick up a stick in the woods. She offers a line that would have inspired any self-infatuated man: "But be not afraid of greatness: some are born great, some have greatness thrust upon them." Men are visionaries, feasting on this woman's beauty.

THE DISCOVERY OF COLETTE

GLENS FALLS HOSPITAL, NY
AUGUST 29, 1996

ON THE NIGHT COLETTE WAS BORN, she looked straight at her father that first second of her life.

She felt at home with his voice; this gave him immense pleasure. Infants need words, just as they need warmth, breast milk, and soft but firm swaddling. He could sense that early on. Yet their need for words is immediate, not deliberate. Adults need words that can last, like a promise. Children can contemplate a vast immediate.

Colette gave him a new reason to contemplate midlife. She was at once glorious, like fuzzy fiddleheads in April about to burst forth. She walked the weekend before her first year, as if the calendar had been calibrated just for her.

When he looked into her patient eyes, he felt that timing was everything. At forty-two, he was indeed prepared to enjoy child-rearing. The ancient Anasazi knew exactly when to plant corn in Chaco Canyon to collect the right amount of sun and rain in the harsh desert light. The birth of Colette was a similar harvest for him and his wife.

Colette was completely herself—and remained that way, to his utter astonishment and stunning satisfaction, forever.

COLETTE AT NIGHT, THE FIRST FOUR YEARS

OLD STONE CHURCH ROAD, 1996 to 2000

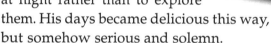

AT NIGHT HE EXCELLED, thinking through the moves of his next business day. This made most of his days prepared and less vulnerable to the passage of time. Perhaps night work kept him from dreaming, as he struggled to resolve things at night rather than to explore them. His days became delicious this way, but somehow serious and solemn.

When he grew near Colette at night, his long-embedded habits changed. He could hear her breathe—a few ounces of air per breath—and the space of that inhale gave way to a new, less prepared, less decisive, more wondrous world. The next day, his darker side would lift some, or even disappear. Memory was mixed with present joy, and it proved different.

Colette at night was close to wonder. She took away his thoughts about what came next. When he woke the next morning, he didn't feel so much refreshed as remade, like a paragraph of prose that gets reconfigured into a poem, or a phrase from a friend restated as pure unqualified praise.

Later, he would remember this phase vividly, and would understand why less selfish couples created mountains of children to surrender to. Eventually, he came to believe that God had granted Varlissima and him a careful compliment.

Colette at night took many things from him, even his health at times, but the exchange of air between them was worth every second from his life.

THE FIRST OBSESSION

RECEIVING TENURE AT RENSSELAER
TROY, NY, 1990s

READING WAS HIS FIRST OBSESSION. Born to disadvantage, but enabled by the grace of good books, reading was to him as basic as breathing. It seldom left his side.

When Colette was about ten, the family had taken a vacation to Portland, Oregon. There, he sat one afternoon with his daughter on a park bench that had, at one end, a statue of a seated man: the man was relaxed, his left ankle resting on his right thigh, and he wore a broad-rimmed hat to protect his face from the sun.

But what stuck in his mind, in finding a photograph from that afternoon, was neither the statue nor the park, nor the pleasure of being with his daughter. What he remembered was that on that bench between him and Colette lay a book.

For years afterward, whenever Colette was away, the image of that book sitting between them would haunt him. Why could he not have sat alone with Colette, in a blinding immediacy?

Half the trouble with this reading obsession came from the ways that good reading came to erase obstacles for him. Reading had reshaped the contours of misfortune in his youth, and then outdistanced his self-doubt upon meeting women like Varlissima. Reading was full of symbolic domination.

The other half of this first and lasting obsession was that it could suspend time. Reading was the only tonic that calmed the speed of time for him. As he sat surrounded by pages, engaged in another's narratives, imagining other lives, suddenly decades would pass, and he would emerge more informed with daughter and wife.

Within a year of having received tenure at Clarkson, he discovered that he disliked the stability—and the threat of stability—so much that he left to work for Mario Cuomo's New York State Energy Research and Development Authority, in 1988 and 1989.

Now, without ever having taken a business class in his life, he was a tenured director at the Lally School of Management and Technology. This recognition of his ability to read and to adapt came to haunt him. Once accepted into a club, he often resisted remaining in the club.

And within a year of receiving tenure at Rensselaer, he left again, only to roam more broadly in his readings. During his decade at Rensselaer, he was often simply astonished how management faculty had no real books on their shelves. They had data that aged. This made him realize that he had to leave the academic setting completely for something else, something more action oriented. With that, he had to leave their world for something, anything else. It was the uncertainty of the game that always seduced him to excel, and it was the certainty of academic schedules that frightened him the most.

ATTIC BLISS

AT HOME ON
OLD STONE CHURCH ROAD, 2009

MEMORY IS A KIND OF ACCOMPLISHMENT. He knew this best from the attic of their home on Old Stone Church Road. In the litter of that attic, he saw everything he had accomplished, and all that he had not. He had some of his best thoughts in that attic, and a few of his worst.

Varlissima had encouraged him to look at dozens of properties before they settled on the white home across from the Old Stone Church. There were dozens of problems with the property, from the flood in the basement to the insects in the attic. But the place spoke to both of them instantly—and they knew that it was lifelong, and they knew it would be a challenge to maintain and improve.

The house was on an ancient site, pre-Revolutionary, from the time of the French and Indian Wars. It was near a pond, with more than a dozen giant maples lining the old carriage route to the Old Stone Church, which was across the street. Most importantly, it was the place where Colette was born, and then grew up.

Colette had now lived in the home for a dozen years. Much time had passed, while she played at archery in the backyard and became a talented athlete. It was already August, and she was about to turn into a teenager before their eyes.

Yet time itself was suspended in the attic: layers of dust dated the gifts. He could remember her complete past, and now worried about her near future.

The rocking chair—that strange, horse-like rocking chair that Colette would ride on for hours—was still there, in the slanted light of the attic. Her Christmas gifts seemed antiques, eyeing her new interests, so suddenly arrived.

Suddenly, he felt he saw two girls from his attic view, each pausing at the window of her bedroom. One was innocence itself; the other stood tall, like a young woman with a bearskin on her skull, like the ancient god Artemis herself. The first, slightly stooped, was nameless and without precedent, seeking safety and security, humbled yet somehow also proud.

Old Stone Church was to the left of this girl's choice, with open, pine-filled woods to the right. He could see both girls in the one girl, and this worried him.

One jumps into the future, and this Colette is lovely in motion, certain in motion, running like a deer, like a reborn Artemis, bow in hand, ready to accept a college scholarship for such balance in running. This is the Colette we can have confidence in. She makes the fall safely into life, matures like the rest of us, and settles well each night into sleep.

But there is another Colette, suspended in her fall, arrested in the worst sense, motionless in the air. And while she is embraced by her father, she is not free to be herself.

She is in pinched quarters like a servant.

She is in a garret like a struggling artist.

She is in a room for a lonely child.

She is in a sanctum without noise and family.

She is behind time, and alone.

She is an image from another life.

This second Colette wrote a letter to Emily Dickinson, who never wrote back to her.

MEETING JAY

MIDDLEBURY, VERMONT, 2008

HE HAD SUSPECTED SINCE HIS CORNELL YEARS that greatness was a state of mind. He remembered first having this thought while taking Professor Laurence Moore's advanced seminar in Madness and Civilization at Cornell. It came to him while reading R.D. Laing's *Knots.*

Now, at age fifty-three, having watched the self-destruction of so many talented as well as so many disadvantaged people, he concluded that it is not boastful to think of yourself as great when you yourself outsmart poverty. This took vigilance, this self-forgiveness past poverty, as much as it took energy and drive. In a way, it justified one's self. It felt great to arrive there, at last. By fifty-three, he had written a *New York Times* bestseller from a state of mind that was his own—how to do more with less. This was his ninth book in thirty years, and it would not prove his last.

During the prior decade, he was leaving the art of writing in black and white, and started trying more colorful things. Blending fiction and nonfiction in his books on business and society was beginning to feel right, and some readers were responding. He then took these thoughts further into the ordinary. For when ordinary things—like the color white or a daughter's smile—become extraordinary, greatness nears again, but this time with more force and fascination. It is a phase, a set of moments, a state of mind that becomes a daily condition, a habit of being, a way to live. The state of reading becomes heightened into a state of writing. The state of longing becomes something that empowers one to strive for more.

Greatness resides in each of us, if tapped with diligence, allowing the developed self to defeat the destructive self. When he looked over so much self-destruction in the lives of creative people in the past, he felt lucky—even at times, great—to have found someone who was a sound family man, and a creative man to boot.

Without having met Jay Parini, however, he would most likely have remained arrested in his own attic of hope and rusted intentions. For most of his life, he had found glimpses of greatness in women, in reading, and in travel. But this time he found it residing in a man.

He met Jay in a moment of sudden rightness, when Colette wasn't yet a woman, and when he was ripe with business, but not yet ripened to write about his own life.

Jay lived on top of a hill outside Middlebury, Vermont, ninety-three miles from the Old Stone Church. He had discovered Jay's books by chance. He had been flipping through the racks of Lyrical Ballad, a used bookstore on Phila Street in Saratoga. The bookstore—a former Adirondack Bank vault—housed a vast collection of used works. He picked up a book by Jay that reminded him of greatness. And this used bookstore gave him Jay for less than five bucks.

After having seen one of Jay's novels made into a fine independent movie, he boldly sent him his new manuscript, which was about Ben Franklin and the art of competitive frugality. He included a short letter praising Jay's film, *The Last Station*, and its tale about two loves: one between a young man and woman, and the other between Tolstoy and his wife—an old lion and his lioness.

Jay invited him in. The trip into Jay's world became a routine: writer to writer, friend to friend.

Jovial in his poems and warm in his person, Jay was the best example of a balanced creative person he had met to date. A man

59

with a mother, a family, and a pile of books to his name, Jay had written beautiful biographies of American giants like Robert Frost and John Steinbeck—big biographies full of warmth, empathy, and good and honest charm.

The first time he returned from visiting Jay, filled with energy and eager to focus on his writing, Colette and Varlissima resorted to exotic idioms to capture what they saw in this meeting of the two men: "It was like dried firewood meeting a flame," Varlissima said, echoing the Chinese phrase for instant attraction.

"No, Mom," Colette dove right in, "Dad's visits with Jay are when things go well. Dad is shaking the skeleton, wiggling his bucket, throwing a foot, getting the moths off, and plucking the turkey—all at once." He felt that the young Colette made remarkable sense, without much pretense.

They both knew, these wise women, that Jay had a kind of warmth in his person and in his prose that was seldom found in the world of normal masculine competition.

Varlissima once accused him of not having enough male friends, and he replied, "Yes, but I have good friendships"—and pointed to a picture of Jay in the woods. The arts of competition were so deep in him that even joy came with some remorse, and even pure friendship had its suspicions.

Once, when some teenagers had roughed up Robert Frost's historic Vermont home, the judge asked Jay, "Can you knock some sense into these kids? They are so lost, and much of what they did was in ignorance of the great man Frost." Jay agreed, and he met with the kids a few times, reading to them and teaching them about poetry.

In reaching Jay's world, he relearned how to leave his world of professional distractions and inconsequential distinctions.

In meeting Jay, he came to a moment of reconciliation with his own ambition. He was ordinary, and that was enough. He was sensual—and that was special. The way forward was to articulate this ordinary specialness that all humans share.

HIS NEIGHBORHOOD
AFTER MEETING JAY

AT HOME ON OLD STONE CHURCH ROAD, 2010

AFTER MEETING JAY, he became again a literary frontiersman. There was a feast before him now, in his books, in his yard, with his family. This shift back to a quiet neighborhood was good, and perhaps great. It was the first time since West Islip he was on his own, away from the obligations of larger organizations. On his own.

The Old Stone Church, originally a jolly good investment, was now igniting his imagination. Backed by his finances as a management consultant, and taking the extra cash from the sales of his books, he had bought the old place, with its church, and his home, and the large Adirondack rooms, and the immense, ready-to-fall barn, at a bargain basement price.

No one in their right mind wanted the obligations of such old property stock at the time, when Saratoga was about to boom with plenty of new building stock. So he bought it at what Ben Franklin would have found a frugal and inventive price.

Now after living in the place in a beat-up condition for the first twelve years of Colette's life, he returned to its historic needs, and made plans with a few builders and architects and engineers. History had kissed his youth, and the many large trees in this property reminded him of the history of this place, so he took the dive into further investment in property improvements, after meeting Jay. He can say with some confidence that he took this dive because he liked how Jay supported his family on top of the hill, where he wrote from in Vermont. And he can say with some wonder that he found many corporate tax deductions the more he invested in its stock. During the Obama years, there may have been no better write-off for small business owners than rebuilding their properties.

The giant oaks that lined the ancient carriage way to the church began to astonish him. Almost the entire time he had been a professor, he had not taken the time to walk that part of the property. Now it was a daily routine, rain or shine, winter or summer. And a kiss to Colette or Varlissima near the tall trees was supernatural, at times.

It was the same now for his trips; he brought the library of his literary ambitions with him on the road now. Whenever he drove to Jay's home, he retraced in his memory the mighty, early American landscape and the equally compelling set of characters that history had brought to his neighborhood during the French and Indian Wars. He hired Ed, a local archeologist and another friend he met through books, to dig around in his basement, and sure enough it was pre-Revolutionary. The basement could be clearly dated to 1770, perhaps to the early 1760s, making it older than all the other stock in Saratoga, including the Old Brian Inn.

He was feeling more a part of history than ever before. From the Old Stone Church, up through central Vermont, he would drive past land mines of memories. Crossing near the Hudson, he would enter a space before the American Revolution, and retrace the contours of its battlefields. There, about thirty miles short of Jay's home, he saw the sharp-eyed Vermont boys fingering their muskets; he felt the deals that had allowed the Six Nations to form the Iroquois Federation.

"Be open to the sun," he heard them say.

"Be bolder," he heard Jay say.

Here he experienced again, in a most sensual fashion, the rivers, lakes, and portages long obscured by modern development, long hidden by his talks of policy and technology at Rensselaer and about Washington, DC. This was no longer talk for talk's sake; this was the action he had always longed for.

Visiting Jay, this American narrative writer, brought a storm of longings back to him: his education, his desire to write new things, the things of his youth that had been neglected during his moneymaking years. Boom. All back.

By the time he arrived in Vermont at the hilltop landing, where Jay's wife practiced as a psychologist, he felt Jay's immediate warmth, and the warmth of his traditions. Each time there, he forgot his brutal, machinelike business successes. He began to read out loud again.

He recalled Henry David Thoreau's breathtaking encounter with the loon, and he thought he could try to write like that someday soon, natural and supernatural, both at once.

After meeting Jay, his neighborhood became as rich as his hand-selected library, each book and tree standing tall as a part, as a delegated and supernatural part, of history. He could now joke with Jay—they were both part of this American tradition of self-invention that stretched from a great like Walt Whitman on Long Island up to Jay in Vermont and now to him, struggling and rewriting every day in the foothills of the Adirondacks. He said to Varlissima, "I guess self-delusion can be such a good thing for a writer, for after tons of it, you develop a skill at self-invention!"

MOBY DICK AFTER MEETING JAY

RETURNING FROM VERMONT TO
OLD STONE CHURCH, 2011

HE WAS NOW IN HIS MIDDLE FIFTIES. How had that happened? Far too fast, he felt. How the hell did this happen so fast? He had spent several decades in an articulated orchestrated delay of youth, like many writers and artists do, or try to do.

But when he felt this turbulence from time within, rather than letting it bring him down, he usually sought to visit Jay. In time, rereading Jay at home even did the trick, and there were over two dozen masterworks to chose from.

After so much preparation, after so much reading, he now knew that he was able to jump only so far up as a writer. Without uttering a single word, Jay, through all of his published words collectively, helped him accept his standing, and proceed as both writer and businessman.

As he reread many classics after the success of *Doing More With Less,* he saw something more than any of his professors would have made him realize during his first days at Cornell: it was the non-narrative chapters in *Moby Dick* that were the most astonishing, like Colette herself.

While the world was taught to appreciate a good story, and always will, some amazing writing can be found in non-narrative passages, like in a talk with a daughter, or during a walk with a wife. He could not have realized how extraordinary great writing is in an ordinary sense until he had fathered Colette, and until he had begun investing in rebuilding his properties. The strange blend of a daughter and a new place to work and write from—a place that was actually ancient, like a classic—began to breed in him a kind of bliss, and a new kind of writing. Rereading these classics proved one of the best ways to beat fatigue, ordinary business travel fatigue, to outlast the daily insult and wear of money-making. He was getting better at doing both, making money and writing.

He'd look out his office window at the hanging sculpture of a copper whale from the New Bedford Whaling Museum swaying in the wind, so bright it would shed reflected light. It reminded him daily of how great Melville was to his mind.

He had taught for seven years at Clarkson "the Great Books curriculum"—Aurelius to Franklin, Whitman, and Melville. Those days spent teaching the greats were a blip compared to now, when he could consume a classic without needing to tell anyone.

Rereading these classics now, away from Cornell, long gone from Potsdam and Troy, was pure pleasure. Márquez's magical *One Hundred Years of Solitude,* the great literature of reality by Tom Wolfe and Gay Talese, the strong histories by Robert Caro—each brought new techniques to his page. He was, at last, preparing himself for a still larger literary world.

Nonetheless, with some strangeness, and that same remorse from poverty in youth, each hour that he spent with a master classic, he felt like he was getting away with murder. He had been trained, born to be a laborer, so this leisure-class pleasure was, in the back of his mind, still perverse. This perversity was a cause of guilt, and the guilt was deeper than guilt, since it involved remorse.

Fate had allowed him so much more: he could sway in the wind like that copper whale. He would attract the light, shine his copper tail. Some of his friends had already been dead a dozen years, like Donald Ferguson, his West Islip neighbor, from a bad liver. Donald was a dear friend who had lived near him and Lillian, closer than the Old Stone Church now stood to his Saratoga home.

Some days it became enough to simply read a classic, watch the wind blow his whale, and think about a bigger writing project. This was unthinkable during the first five decades of his life. But now, after meeting Jay, it was not only possible, it was increasingly probable each day. Somehow he felt it would eventually prove profitable, like his prior decades of business facilitation and deal-making. Ironically, when he'd weigh back in with his staff about their consulting or business outreach projects, he discovered his firm had leaped ahead without his micromanagement. His firm was growing despite his not always being there.

His ascent, he felt, had been unfair to others, and yet everyone thought he had earned it. That was what was magical about wealth: one cannot get wealth alone; it descends from others. That was the new paradox he was learning from the classics. Another thing became clear: it is in the longing for something great that one comes to understand the moments of supreme fiction in a life. To be fair, it was a number of thinkers who taught him this: from Aurelius to Márquez, from Franklin to Parini, it took a long village of books to make this new point sink home. It is the words themselves that amaze in a marriage—not plot, nor simple surfaces, nor the dramas we make with our mates. This is how he chose to make the ordinary extraordinary. The story line becomes sublime. The setting makes the ordinary extraordinary.

This deeper sense of self in every reader is neither coastal nor oceanic, neither rich nor poor. It is universal. It is sublime. It is inclusive. It is like an apricot: sensual, made of curls and curves, made to delight.

Leaving Jay one day, he said, "Every writer needs to write for that apricot." Take, for example, the entire chapter Melville wrote on the color white! He could get lost in all its twists and turns. He was glad that Melville's publisher had been too busy, or too intimidated, to edit this chapter much. Like genius itself, the chapter was best left alone. He had tried to allow the same with Colette.

In this passage he felt all the seasons of Melville's mind. Yet the chapter did not move forward: it was not based on a protagonist, did not relate at all to Ahab or Ishmael. The chapter stood on its own: self-contained, magnificent and worthy of occupation. The passage brought him back to that first moment he saw Colette.

Right then and there, he came to understand that Melville had written about white in all its contrasting magnificence. Melville's white was different from, but exactly like, a young girl's face. It was the white of his daughter's face. It was a white of standing in a life.

He concluded something by reading all the works by Jay Parini, as he had read all the works he could find of Walt Whitman: Life is richest when interrupted, when the colors of life are neither exaggerated nor muted, but exact.

The baby cries, the milk spills, the knees scrape. Being attentive to the unaccomplished is its own form of richness.

APPRECIATING VARLISSIMA

OLD STONE CHURCH,
SOMEWHERE BETWEEN 1999 and 2010

THIS TRADITION OF MARRIAGE STUNS, and proves more stunning with each decade together. A bee's sting bites, but what's stunning about marriage is that the parties do not die from the stings. Instead, a marriage's honey keeps oozing after the wound smarts and burns, as the expectations become memories and the patterns become who you are with each other.

Appreciating Varlissima was about becoming both male and female, inland and coastal, father and husband, classic and ordinary. She had given him his first primal glimpse of the moments that outlast time, such as when a child is brought into the world.

They had met on a mountaintop of passion—sweet, sensual, apricot-like passion. She had just left her teens, a remarkably smart and experienced woman with red hair.

Back then, in the 1980s, she was the best at what he wanted, and he could not comprehend anything other than what he wanted when near her. As their second and then third decade drew to a close, they became more like lovers and friends. Memory is the magic in accomplishment, a source of renewal, and the things bred from good memories prove to be the things that allow further life. By their third decade together, they were both ready to leave youth.

Colette was born in 1996, in the middle of their second decade. She made him realize that all his little life crises were inconsequential compared to her birth.

It was easy to be with Varlissima as a parent. Her entire Sicilian-American culture asked of them nothing less than this. Her entire set of genes insisted each day and night on exactly this. The early days—Colette's first days at junior high school, the sweet suspended sixteen years she spent with her girlfriends before college—took on a new glow in his memory after meeting Jay.

Somehow, gratefully, he was now able to carry those good memories—as he stumbled forward, entering a long period that he called "the sensual middle."

PART TWO

THE SENSUAL MIDDLE

"I have acquired a very few notions only on
what is better not to put in a book.
Paint only what you have seen. Look for a long time
at those things that give you pleasure,
still longer at those things that give you pain.
Try to be faithful to your first impression.
Don't make a fetish of the 'rare word.'
Don't tire yourself with lying."

—COLETTE
PREFACE TO *AUX ILES DE LA LUMIÈRE*

Prelude

Experience and Middle Age

PART TWO IS ABOUT FEAR AND LONGING. In addressing these fears, Bruce found a confidence that comes with successful repetition.

The mystery of middle age is that one's fears reshape themselves as vivid memories, while some wriggle beyond that reshaping like a snake sheds its skin. We remember ourselves in the blind basement of youth, in the many dark alleys that taught us how we were to live—this process of recollection and growth is primal and purposeful, almost automatic. Yet we also long for more, much more, knowing there will be so much less.

As we age, we learn how not to tire ourselves with youthful lying, how to do much more with less. These middle-age fears often strengthen the drive and hunger to succeed in strange and rich ways. Sometimes these fears terminate or slow down a life. But in his case, they accelerated the search for meaningful action.

The poet William Carlos Williams argues that memory is "a kind of accomplishment." This poetic rendition of what we all experience through the long plateau of middle age matters. In middle age we can enjoy a remarkable valley, a sameness if you will, that is so different from the lust and bursts of youth, so unlike the medical visits and acid preparations for death in old age, that it feels like an accomplishment. There is a long afternoon possible, in the ambitions of middle age.

Williams proved more than poetic, in fact, offering in one phrase a psychological insight that betters those of Freud and Jung and Erickson. For if "memory is an accomplishment" there is nothing boastful and nothing unnecessary in Bruce telling readers how he outmaneuvered youthful trauma and pain. For in remaking our lives, we reinvent our friends, reshape our families, and in his case, structure a firm.

By middle age, he had wrapped enough thought around the events of his small and faulted life, even when he knew that the most important relationships were born randomly, even when he accepted how arbitrary business success proves. Middle age can make the missing whole, as it makes the spent fresh. And all this we feel as luck and magic, knowing that the end could be so near.

From Edwin Torres and Suie Yin Chang to those who depended on his continued business success, from Hurricane Sandy to the remarkable jokes of Varlissima, from being fatherless to becoming the father, he pulled these strands of meaning from youth. *Youth never leaves us if we know how best to make it a set of lasting memories.* He spun these tales like the silk fabric of an awaiting spider. This fabric became the higher facts of life.

He found, after so much grounding, that we cannot excavate our lives in a manner both alert and tender using only toothpicks. This kind of memoir requires mental trucks as large as those that excavate ore or oil or the taconite pellets we forge into steel in America's Midwest, and ship on the Great Lakes of our stories.

In the same way that the faithful are blessed with a sense of inscrutable purpose, despite a universe of blinding complexity, youth is the best and the only high-octane start for a memoir. *Those who have the greatest lives are often those who allow the memories of youth to dominate.* Yet middle age is the time when we make meaning of it all, or die desperate and unfulfilled.

He learned one thing about middle life: memory by then is more massive than identity. He had conquered youth, and with it, some significant fears. But by middle age, a boatful of fears remained past simple conquest, such as:

Fear that the death of his father would continue to depress.
Fear that the death of his mother would bring him into the realm of an orphan.
Fear that success in business might narrow and make hollow his love of words for their sheer sake.
Fear that in time, his ability to bring joy and the touch of good fortune to others might fester and decay.

In retrospect, he now realized that he even feared the wondrous valor of women. Except in rare cases of dignity, he began indulging these fears because many women now had a power over him, an ability, if mean and petty, to evaporate his uniqueness into something more polished, and acceptable, and sweet, and near death. They were making him civilized, and he needed to resist this at times to remain or to become more creative. Being a sheep was not to his liking.

He was not a five-star general, but a simpler soldier.
He was not a father of many, but of one.
He was not surrounded as much by enemies, as by these fears.
He had a constant fear that the future was more like a flooding than the sun-rich nuance of youth's coasts and adventures.

Bruce spent many days trying to prevent the boat of these fears from capsizing. While he remained generous in allowing many to hop in with him, he sometimes simply wanted to hop out of this long valley of middle age.

THE ART OF BEING A DOG

HE HAD ONCE KNOWN A DOG NAMED ZACHARY. Zach would limp for affection and attention. He might be sniffing the ground, but he was always eyeing something better. Zach was a fantastic dog, warm and fuzzy, smart and tenacious.

Nonetheless, he was easily distracted by a new smell or a new thought; even squirrels could change instantly his calculating equation—and he'd sprint off, forgetting the limp that had gotten him noticed in the first place.

In youth—and even in middle age—there were so many ways in which he felt like Zach, felt himself exactly like a dog. For years, he thought this was because he had come into the world poor, with little advantage except his senses and wit, but now he knew better.

Colette thought that her Dad-man had been a bear in another life, "Because you protect your cubs, and because you are big and cuddly." Not really, he thought—the deeper, less romantic truth was that he was a dog. No adults really felt him to be a bear, and while he loved his young Artemis daughter, he felt that she exaggerated his size and reach.

His animal spirit was reflective of his deep nature. What was funny was that they, the public, kept feeding him, prompting him. Opponents on the basketball court, whenever he caught them in a fake, called him a dog; early business partners—like Robin, who had owned paintings by Rembrandt—paused when he'd bought them out, to call him a dog. When he met his investors' obligations and left the world of debt before age forty, some had called him un-American—but most had called him, behind his back, "another white Cornell-bred dog." They were usually from the better breed of schools like Harvard, INSEAD, the London School of Economics, or the Manchester School of Business—and their deans and faculty had come from similar pedigrees. He took no offense; but as he did on the basketball court, he chose to make their offense the object of his skill.

Why had it taken him so many decades to accept the obvious? God had granted him a dog's curiosity since his birth in that home near the railroad tracks. Nothing more, little less. Yet it was nothing short of hilarious and gracious and good that the big men and the big women in society kept rewarding him for being dog-like.

At church, a minister asked that the social progressives in his community become like boa constrictors—"We need you to be bold, open, and affirmative! Amen! That is our calling in life. Be a boa—offer yourself to a life of action for the good."

Bruce felt that the metaphor of being a good dog was much more convincing. He was afraid to tell his minister this. He knew to go with what interested him, until something even better roamed before him. Having survived a rather turbulent youth, he thought: "You can always go back to the original smells, and find a place to leave your mark."

He began thinking that the good deals that had granted him privilege had resided somewhere in his brain before they became real. This was his most fascinated thought since the birth of his daughter—spunk was in him all along, and it was about learning to let it out. Many spoke of the importance of self-esteem, others about self-worth, and a few more missionaries harped about the certainty of wealth as a sign of divine obligation. This all seemed a bit elevated in his mind, for he knew business to be pedestrian, and success a collection of white scattered bones.

Dante taught him that most lives are more a divine comedy than some stately sequence. His position between the inferno of self-interest and the hells of business and literary accomplishment were punctuated by many adventures in realms of more pleasant, heavenly things, such as the smile of a girl or the chase of a dog in the park. Each peak of pleasure seemed to matter more as he aged, and memories came in the scent of a woman, in the muddy trail of a deal, in running so fast that he sometimes ran right over the petrified squirrels he was chasing.

Memory was stored like the smells in a dog—by intensity, by category, and in a vast and complex system of recall.

After the discovery of Colette, he began to dig deeper, sniffing around a bit, to see what was still out there.

EXTENDING A LIFE

DIGGING DEEPER INTO HIS MEMORIES OF
CORNELL AND WEST ISLIP, A NEW CENTURY

WHEN VARLISSIMA FIRST MET HIM AT CORNELL in the early 1980s, and watched him gain the attention of an entire room at an art reception in the Johnson Museum, she said he was like "a wet dog, coming in from the cold, shaking. And the funny thing is, Bruce, you're aware you are shaking water all over the well-dressed and ambitious folks, those third- and fourth-generation Cornell people who've become so certain, so calcified. Hell, they laugh with you, as if you were pissing on them to assuage their sins. But you do it in such a loveable, predictable way, that they love you. Damn it, Bruce. How did you learn to do that?"

This was the moment he first paused to fall in love with Varlissima. She knew from the start something about him that took him decades to discern.

In any case, something deeper than self-interest emerged in his sense of what others sensed about him. Whenever he got the whiff of something special, he was rapidly all over it. This instinct to sniff things out for the better is what really extended his life from youth.

This thought became a feeling for him, a habit that allowed him to watch anger, love, dread, and fear hit the keyboard of others in business meetings, while he remained himself—the proud, open dog. Zeal, persistence, self-control, the supreme pleasure of self-motivation—these were the rich, turbulent sources of will and character. A good dog understands as much, so why not man? This thought path proved more profitable than business training, as it was explosive.

But where, exactly, in his neighborhood, did these important, doglike attributes of his own self-determination reside? Was it his forcefulness that had given rise to success? Or perhaps success in business, as in life, is a by-product of these primal forces in each of us, waiting to be unleashed on some sunny afternoon, during a walk with the things one comes to love? The emotional mind, neighbor to the soul, is associative. That is what made him possible, all this probable, his life meaningful.

He would ask her—this woman before him—a question, and her answer would be rich in detail and associations, but not fact. He felt at home with this from his days with his mother, a richly associative woman. They would walk the neighborhood, with their dog Kahlil, a black lab whose tail was permanently twisted from being slammed in a kitchen door (he still shuddered at the thought of that slamming door). He concluded that he would never feel better in his life—in the full warmth and the glow of sincere attention—than when he walked with Kahlil and his younger mother in the afternoon light.

This realization meant much to him; it was more emotional than mathematical, more about the self that enabled business and success than the success in business. The older he got, the more he celebrated his doglike conquests. How was this possible for a fellow born so poor?

Well, he began to give himself a crash course in human development. Turns out that the neocortex of the human brain sits outside and around the amygdala and the thalamus. That's a fact, in all cases—from liars to billionaires, from Casanova to Jonathan Edwards, and to other churchgoers and the doers whom he had always admired. *What distinguished the dog-like was not allowing cultivation and civilization to snip off the contacts with those inner organs.* What allowed his kind of business success in life was probably based on not being repressed. He returned his attention to the works of Freud and his many followers, preferring those with a brain research slant to their claims, those who thought about the mind the way a neurologist does. It was so much more primal than the calculations of risk and benefit.

For an outside stimulus can sometimes travel along a back alley—past the everyday, cultivated self—allowing the amygdala, deep in the brain, to receive a direct message from the senses. Dogs understood these back alleys instinctively, as did the best of the leaders Bruce advised. Dogs know, as he somehow knew, where the best treats were—even after having gorged himself silly on some treats right before their eyes. He'd share these findings freely. In this way, he was a little different from Zachary and Kahlil.

He tried, then, after his first millions in business, to figure out what made him enterprising. The response to a certain kind of stimulus occurs *before* any thoughts have registered in the hotel of the neocortex. This is not about business plans, or formal loans, or structured strategies, and what he told his staff to call "the logic of growth" had to be primal if it was to be real. This was about passion, the passion of being human, and the focus of those passions along the lines of question-based marketing. When you arrive at that point, with the squirrel within striking distance, you feel the moment special—and you want those moments again and again. These are moments when consequence is not even contemplated. These are moments of high emotional significance, and ultimate salvation.

In this way, his business drive and his life as a writer were tied. They became one—his mother and father, his soul and his bank accounts.

He could see these moments of sudden rightness, these feelings of primal want, in the steel-black eyes of his loveable dog. Kahlil would love him without condition—and always did, for seventeen years. Even when he could no longer walk the block, Lillian called Kahlil a "rug runner" to save his pride. He would love his business with the same force of longevity.

Yet the point beneath these vivid memories remains that look seeking affection: it is the look of wanting, that pitiful look of needing attention that establishes the value in a dog's life. What matters is that the dog understands the back alleys and the limelight. And what matters to all who love him are those moments when his steel eyes look up, and he sees something better on the horizon.

Digging deeper into his memories of West Islip and of his decade at Cornell, he realized he had been that successful dog from day one. It was about having survived youth for a longer stage. It is ironic that it took society so long to catch up to him.

In his case, business success was more about an arrival into middle age: his authentic, loveable, actual self—despite the drool that sometimes dripped from his jowls as he made his way to the bank. As he returned a ball of enthusiasms for his lady, as he satisfied another big client, he felt a doglike pride. It was not calculating in any formal or fashionable sense. It was not planned; it was primal. If he had a tail, he would be wagging it daily—from behind the podium, and during and after work. He had always been good at living over time, but now as he edged sixty, he was beginning to understand why.

THE SENSUAL
CERTAINTY OF YOUTH

ANYWHERE IN THE WORLD, BUSINESS
MEETINGS WITH THOUGHTS HELD INSIDE

THE SENSUAL CERTAINTY OF YOUTH still churned in him, even as he aged. It made him sense each day as an opportunity. He did not find himself lost in the middle of life like Dante. Instead, he found himself consumed by the middle of life. He was now a businessman, the owner of a self-made corporation, and it consumed his hours like a moth is consumed by light. He was teaching during those first decades, and publishing, but in retrospect, it was business that preoccupied his days. Even in the middle of most semesters, he was somewhere else, building staff, renting offices, doing deals. He was the deal-maker, not the professor.

Business was this moth, his moth, a serious yellow-tailed moth, with large green eyes on its wings. This moth of serious distraction flapped its zigzag ways into consuming a life, his life, much of his middle life, as it gave him a sense of mission, a purpose, a stage that seemed to grow each night, expand each city, evolve into a global exchange. A business-based day proved much easier than the anxiety inherent in fine writing. He would use his classes to entertain himself and the students with some of his findings, but he would use his life to profit from the learning. The moth kept growing in its intensities.

Yet the truth is always about the same light, this game called business. Over time, he started thinking past the incentives and disincentives, and paid attention to the music that was being played during each deal. Whether he was dealing in Europe, Africa, Asia, or Canada, the music was always the same. It was Igor Stravinsky's "Circus Polka" that kept churning in his mind, ever youthful, and he was the self-appointed circus master, in a bright red Polish suit, leading the group. While he held the whip, he was also captive to it—as a moth circled his head with profit and ceaseless feasts and temptations.

Why is this fitting? Well, when you grow up poor, it is nearly impossible to resist the moth. Have you ever noticed how hilarious even the best dogs look when running to chomp down a moth? In retrospect, looking over his decades in business, he could now see himself in that posture, a dog ready to chomp down the next moth. Month after month, the next moth hovers. Opportunity is sweet, and she is a self-consuming clown's assistant.

As he aged, however, more tomorrows became deeper than the trauma that had first shaped him. It was in the pursuit of business that he outran his deeper demons, and avoided a tendency to the depressive. He did not die early like his father, as expected! He did not pause to count his wounds when he lost. This was not wisdom. Instead, it was a funny early indication that wisdom in one's life is not only discernible, but also achievable and superb. Eyes can track the moth when you look up; stupidity is trying to kill the moth. He began to ease off some from his chase, but when he realized this, he had already run through much of the world.

Human understanding was not so much about repression, the swatting down of the moths. It was more about subtle alignments to track the moth, until it settled on what mattered. This path of thought lacked rigor. Still it was liberating. In any adventure, you can control the explosions of effort, your limited energy allotments, by a simple alignment with restraint—just by doing more with less. He was becoming an old dog with new tricks, with sharpened skills.

Oddly, as if in a bad joke, he, the born reader and born egotist, was becoming more social. His failings were the failures of humanity, not just his own. It was no longer fair for him to fault himself for being too impersonal. His business success in Africa and Canada depended clearly on the persistence of these attributes. How was all this travel and work even possible?

He began taking an inventory of some key episodes in his life to see if he'd be able to maintain a consistent dog-like worldview. For the one truly beautiful thing about most dogs is that they are not distracted by endless horizons; they know and want home.

He remembered one episode when he was a teenager quite vividly. He was at the seedy bagel place on Oakwood Avenue, across from the bank Lillian used. One of his Hispanic classmates, in a torn T-shirt, suddenly appeared, pulled a knife, and held it beneath his neck simply because he had parked his bicycle in the boy's space. In youth, he did not know how to react to such threats without wanting to kill in self-defense. But being stoic, he did not react—and that may have proved the magic to his survival that day.

Now he saw what happened that day as part of life, from a more restful valley of hope. He felt for that kid, so tortured, so limited in his life, and did not think wrong of him any longer. In fact, he realized that the experience had actually made him stronger.

He remembered clearly the moments when his foster brother Edwin Torres left West Islip to return to Spanish Harlem, then sprinted from his biological family's crowded apartment to Puerto Rico, where he would marry at age sixteen. He did not understand that then. Why marry so young, he wondered? It seemed all too young for his brother to do that. Back then, it felt like a dagger in his heart, an abandonment of Lillian and him.

Now he saw it as part of Edwin's culture, his integration back into Puerto Rico, and understood enough to forgive Edwin. He felt the foolishness now, his foolishness and pride, not Edwin's. There was this strange acceptance in review.

He remembered vividly when Suie Yin Chang left for adoption in California. The sudden feeling of change for Terry, his sister, was overwhelming. Terry cried several Sundays in a row at church. He felt helpless again. Not many families experience the loss of so many children, a father, and a grandmother. And all this—in the first fifteen years of life!

Now he understood this as a useful part of child development. He would meet many competitors in his life, but only a few had this kind of training. It was simply an understatement to call this street smarts.

The missing persons of his life were now taking on a sensual and special certainty. They were the certainty of his survival, the benefits in the risks he took daily now, in bigger and bigger leagues, with larger and larger returns. In youth, risks seemed to invade his mind, risks from Mary Beth in the abandoned home to Sally in the basement. In middle age, they seemed to explain his mind, and his hungry behaviors.

And, of course, he remembered the last day with his father . . . and when Lillian left him for good so suddenly. He remembered the phone call from Terry that Lillian was dying. The anxious flight to Florida only to find her gone.

These events still pained him. They made him the businessman and writer that he was. They only hurt when he breathed. Anywhere he went, the central and sensual certainty of youth was behind him—and for this, he received abundant recompense.

HIS FATHER GLIMPSED IN ISTANBUL

ISTANBUL, TURKEY, 2008

THAT DAY IN TURKEY WAS MISTY. The Bosphorus let off steam as it had on the day that Constantinople had first fallen, in 1453. The hairs on his arm were standing, electric, as if a storm would soon be joining the steam.

He was in Istanbul on one of his many business trips. He had been there often enough not to get lost in the seven hills. There was something fresh in Istanbul's union of East and West—something forgiving, cluttered with opposites, and beautiful. He sensed in Istanbul, as he did in Africa, that he was in a part of the world that was on the rise.

He had been sitting at an outdoor café doing some paperwork, when suddenly he caught a glimpse of a man coming out of a shop who looked exactly like his father. In a near-hypnotic state, he gathered up his papers and began following this man, who reminded him so much of his dad. As he walked behind him, he began to reminisce, remembering how much he missed his father. In actuality, he had spent less time with his dad than he had with many of his business associates. But now, he projected intense feelings associated with his father onto this observed stranger—imagining the way he talked and even the way he walked these seven hills.

Even the posture of this man said, "You're going to miss me when I'm gone." Bruce could almost hear him whispering this remorse in English. "I've taken the high road in this short life," and "I know it must hurt you, Bruce, that I am so remote.

But you have done a good job of looking for me—and father-ing yourself."

This trip had taught him something about his longing for his father and about his home. For years, every man in a military uniform had reminded him of the uniforms in his father's attic. The strange World War II medals—the confusing awards for serving in the Pacific—were anointed by the oils of his fingertips. The absolute silence of relatives, except when talking about rank and the larger mission, began to bother him, even when he was in places like Turkey. These things made him wonder what his father was really like.

In the end, the only evidence he had was military evidence— damn it; he had never found anything more personal than that. But here in Istanbul, the look in the man's brown eyes was the look of his father's eyes. Before the man disappeared into the crowd, he said once more, "You will miss me when I am gone, even when I am young, even when you are old."

This proved one of the most enjoyable and forgiving memo-ries of his middle years. There was no blame in meeting his father.

A missing father can become a perfect father: without harm, without wrongs, full of feelings.

DIVINE COMPENSATION

KYOTO, NARA, AND TOKYO, LATE 1990s through 2012

WITH HIS FATHER NOW SETTLED IN HIS MIND, he began to ask a deeper set of questions about his life. He had taken many flights to Japan, China, and Hong Kong for both business and pleasure. He had toured places in the Far East and the southern hemisphere, like Costa Rica and its neighboring sisters, for equal and engaging reasons. In all of these trips, there was a recurrent pattern, a deeper sense of purpose, but it was during the trips to Asia that this sense of soul searching really stood out.

He began to ask why the artist in him, something he had repressed for business pleasures for so long, continued to work throughout his life rather secretly, rather furtively, and then bloomed in public in his later years. He felt it vividly with each return to Japan, where every inch has been framed, designed, made into art.

This much he knew: He knew he and Varlissima were late bloomers in terms of their devotion to themselves and to family. This stranger devotion to the craft and art of writing was not how he was perceived by most of his friends, business partners, and clients for decades, nor was it how he and Varlissima thought of themselves. They were the son and daughter of laborers. Bruce thought of himself, in particular, more as a wordsmith in action, a facilitator of events, of impact, not texts. He thought of his books as contracts, not art.

He started to notice that, silently, across decades, he and Varlissima had brought the art of his travels back into their home, and into his places of work. He first noticed this one day when staring at a small bronze statue of a deer that stood on the mantel over his office fireplace. The deer's proud stance reminded him of what was best in Colette, and what might prove best in him.

This rediscovery took dominion everywhere in his life, like that proud deer on the mantel. He now felt it the divine compensation for having grown up so poor. He was trained to inspect with driven eyes and cheap tools the nature of things free before him. It was the art in a flower, or a friend, or a lover that defined him, not the pretense or the artifact. He did not need to get deeply involved with things that exercised his talents of observation and delight. He acted within like an artist, without like a businessman. This was possible with Japanese businessmen, so why not bring that atmosphere home?

Turning fifty-six, he reread Marguerite Wilderhain's *The Invisible Core,* her book on pottery published in 1976 and reviewed by him at Cornell, when he last felt himself an artist. Besides E. F. Schumacher's *Small Is Beautiful,* he felt this a life-directing book, found at the right key pivot point in his life, and offering a journey that helped him to reconcile his early ambitions and the world. He could recite, throughout life and in the many classes he taught, word by word this passage that meant so much to him:

> *There is no reason to be proud of whatever gifts one has. They are by the grace of God and not the results of our merits. But there is a reason to be deeply grateful for them, and this gives one the responsibility to use these gifts to the utmost. And not only for ourselves. The more capacity a person has, the greater and more cogent will be the moral obligation to do something honorable with what he has. . . .*
>
> *Let us look at the implication. Man, like all animals, is by nature lazy, but the creative man would always work. He works not only because he wants to create, but because he unconsciously acknowl-*

edges his ability to do so with the acceptance of deeper human respon-
sibility. He understands that his work-time cannot be what it is for
most men, from a certain hour to another definite hour. His work hours
will be his total life, no less. That he feels to be the least he can do to
make up for the gift of abilities that he was given.

He felt this to be the best passage on divine compensation he ever came across in prose. All the others, and there were many, he had come across at the theatre, or in poems, or during speeches he had witnessed by good fortune—and they were therefore more difficult to share with the same businesslike exactness. Although he had never met Wilderhain, he certainty understood what she meant by devotion. He had always felt devoted.

Some travel from boredom, some acquire art because they can. He came to see that his long delay in developing the artist within him was a positive attribute; it protected him like that deer on his mantel. He was there because he was, and nothing more. There was a divine compensation in this. This was shared with Varlissima, and it became a glowing part of Colette, who, explicitly gifted as a visual artist, never suffered the pretense beneath the gifts.

SURPRISE IS NEVER AN ISOLATED EVENT

BEHIND THE OLD STONE CHURCH, 2007

WHAT BEGAN AS A NORMAL WALK, eventually led them behind the Old Stone Church. There was something about the way he and Varlissima looked during their walks that others viewed as romantic, even when they were agitated with each other. During this particular walk, a spy plane might have detected the extra static between their clasped fingers. For she had chosen a spot where only drones could see them. No neighbors were in sight, no horses from nearby farms, no deer among the trees.

There was something precise about her right now, as there had been years before, when she had decided she wanted to conceive Colette—something more magical than demanding, something elastic and wanting. Suddenly she stopped and turned to him, her eyes meeting his. She was smiling that smile—the one that spoke volumes. *"She is a darling and a daring one, after all,"* he thought.

He wondered what angel of mercy had granted them this sudden immediacy—after so many harsh words, and so much fighting over who should be on top. For a moment, he wondered whether this had happened before. Perhaps during the Civil War, when returning soldiers had quick meetings behind the church.

The suddenness of her approach was surprising, and brought him both spiritual and physical joy. Was he about to experience, once again, a moment of sudden rightness with her?

The air was picking up its magic; he could feel the growing breeze from their home across the way. Far from the familiarity of

92

their bedroom, their bodies were still a perfect fit, even after all these years.

She was smooth. He was not.

He gently touched her eyebrows, pushing the hairs in the wrong direction, as he had done a thousand times. But this time, he could smell the long, thick Sicilian hair more clearly and more sharply than ever. Time seemed to stop. *"An entirely new humanist movement could grow from this kind of moment,"* he thought. Each strand of her long thick hair took on a closeness, a scent that filled and fulfilled, as he swirled it into his own personal curl.

There were a thousand reasons the wind was now blowing on them, with them, behind that church. It was his past rushing over her present, and it didn't matter who was winning. In this game of infinite variety, each of them won more than was anticipated or expected. There were tens of thousands of reasons that they were both beyond reason right now, beyond calculation, beyond family obligation. The money tree was swaying, as if to say, "Good deal. Smart move, you two—still connected after all these years."

Her movements lingered like life itself.

He would want that again, he thought. He was almost ready to retreat, but he did not withdraw.

She began again slowly, perhaps sensing that the first time had been too fast. As she moved above him he understood, more than ever before, the Bard's phrase: "I count myself in nothing else so happy." Although her actions lasted but a few moments, he would dream about them for decades.

Trying to establish pace, trying to create tempo, they had become a creative force that felt utterly right. Hovering above him, she reframed his understanding of eternity, and gave more gravity to their shared hopes.

His heart was still pounding. Strangely, his thoughts turned to an image he had once seen of a French library that housed ancient documents—documents that had been well preserved. He felt like one of those documents: alive and alert, and exceptionally lucky to have survived so long.

He began to nod off. She stood watch over him, as she had always done. Then slowly she began moving again, awakening him. There was a remarkable array of feelings in her every move. As the pleasures of their mutually assured second round mounted, the tail on the pollywog in the pond across the way suddenly became a tall organ with an articulate voice. Together, they found this hilarious. He echoed the frog with a keen, primal sound that came from beneath his throat, deep within his chest. She echoed his sounds with a breath that felt primal, ancient. There was a dignity about her, and a strange persistence liberated within him. He explored the unique features of her ears and her mouth, and her fingers gently traced the decades-old scars on his arms from youthful sports injuries.

His heart was pounding a bit less now. He was getting used to their coupling, and somehow feeling more innocent, more accepting of all that she was. They were a couple of consequence, sharing a deep, profound love.

Each book he imagined in that French library was now dressed in lavender leather and stood alone, pulsing with meaning, bringing blood to the forehead and each finger of its many readers. Of the two of them, only Varlissima knew French—and during their intimate exchange, he felt that he wanted to hear her speak French inside his soul. He told her as much. She smiled again that smile.

She was not done, however. She wanted to give him something more than books, something beyond even their shared decades and the home and family they had created. Books matter, but they age. Only the imagination of a couple is real—reliable. And only memory could make an event like this last.

Famous for a few minutes behind the Old Stone Church, he now had everything. Surprise is never an isolated event.

GRANTING HIMSELF FORGIVENESS

RETURNING TO HIS OFFICE, 2008 to 2014

AFTER SO MUCH PLEASURE followed much thought. The dignity of Varlissima resided in a simple principle: she was following an ancient path to him.

His acknowledgement of such an ancient path was counter to all his prior thoughts about Varlissima. She had been the arch of civilization for him, the backbone of a modern woman—well educated, and deliberate in all things.

She had been the ballast against his mindlessness, the caution to his persistence, the eloquent reminder of all things that mattered. Was there a new animal now living in his home, resting like a cougar, ready to pounce beside him as he slept? Would he ever rest properly again? Would she leave him for a younger man, as soon as Colette had left him for college? The feeling of abandon and confusion was profound after so much bliss. Was he too old for her new passions?

It is profoundly unfair when a man ages as a woman blooms.

According to the neuroscientist Joseph LeDoux, the amygdala, the fun center of the brain, matures with speed and fascination quickly in the infant.

Many potent emotional memories are thereby formed in a brain shaped first by the exacting squirts of the amygdala. The church took on new colors, as did his examination of his own brain. He could feel this organ, this juicy apricot, working in new ways as he thought about where to store the meaning of the actions behind the church.

This experience was simply better housed in the amygdala than the neocortex. Up to the encounter at the church, so many years after they had met and married and raised Colette, he had been able to file most of his memories of Varlissima in the neocortex. In this way, they were a proud, civilized couple. But he was filtering through his options now, to find the right space to place this new Varlissima.

He would not be hurried here. He must slow down and relish this into some learning. There were a number of fundamental things about his life that he had to resolve before he could move forward regarding Varlissima.

She had inspired, he was sure, without any intent, this new turmoil in his soul. Even a boy, even a dog, must do certain things in sequence, in order not to offend the gods of routine. He was struggling more now, after the experience, than he had during it.

Would he ever be able to erase, for example, the moment when he realized that his childish attempts to wake his father on that April Fool's Day morning were failing miserably—as Walter, the soldier, spit blood caused by the hemorrhage in his brain? This question still pressed behind his eyes in a fiercely palpable way. Some felt his fears metaphysical. He knew them to be physical.

It was worth several attempts at a full answer. Traumatic events, like the death of his father, had burned into his brain with a fierce imprecision—as if an acid had been used wildly, instead of the neurotransmitters' precise inscriptions.

But when he returned to those back alleys with hope, zeal, and focused deliberate pleasures, he could see that beneath the fear and the blame rested a positive struggle. He had filled his offices with shelves of books trying to understand. He had hired the best lawyers, the best staffers, and had invited some of his best friends to his offices, to surround him during these times of immense stress and uncertainty.

Perhaps just as he had one daughter, it was enough to experience one surreal, super-extended afternoon with Varlissima, and call it a life. The wheels of his recall behind the church kept churning.

Rather than cheapening the primacy of the experience with Varlissima by discussing it out loud, like a hilariously anxious Woody Allen with his psychologist or rabbi, he chose to put the experience, the shocking immediacy of it, into his memory in a fashion deeper than order—as one might place at the front of the mind the higher facts of history.

He came to conclude that the event behind the church that day was a turning point, a moment of sudden rightness. It helped him realize the extent of his self-hatred. It resides in a remorseful recollection that he could not prevent his father's death. This childish sense of forbidden empowerment, this fantasy that a child would and could help was what the scene behind the church helped create, in a cascading sense of forgiveness. He had denied himself so much pleasure until he had figured this out.

FORGIVENESS IS A JOURNEY

CHOOSING ANCIENT PATHS

THE DAY AFTER HIS SURPRISING EN-
COUNTER with Varlissima, he hung a
deep black wooden African mask near
his front office door. That was long ago,
but he still stood near it a few seconds
upon his entry to work each day. The
door was magnificent, with long thin
sheets of window from top to bottom
on each side, so he had a great view of
the outside from the inside. But he
chose to hang the mask just inside the
door, like a hidden totem, so people would be able to see it only
upon entry. This way, he could contemplate the darkness of
ancient ways before he met another day at his computer. This
dark energy was what had settled continents.

The dark African mask assumed some real power in his office.
It suggested that he might be able to reach his reset button again,
to pretend again that the day was completely new. But he knew
he had been transformed by Varlissima once again. It wasn't completely his life, no matter how self-centered he had feigned to be.
Transfiguration was the right word, and it fixed his many wrongs.
It enabled him to walk on stilts in the muck of his actual life,
skipping through the worst thickets into a smoldering realm of
higher fact.

Was this the same kind of mental dance that the ancients had
found useful in ritual dramas? At least half of his library collec-

tion had been assembled to answer this question about ritual and history.

Some 5,000 years ago, when the last of the men and women had crossed the frigid Bering Strait to a lush new world, had they relied on the same set of skills in order to survive the harsh elements of their crossing?

There were two further lessons in this experience turned transfiguration. By middle life, he had found that the hippocampus and the neocortex are merely the well-paid handlers of the mind, the PR professionals of the self. They do everything they can to justify, to rationalize, as we say.

However, he chose in this case not to overpay, and overplay, these PR pros. He would not allow these pulses to be framed as a midlife crisis. That was too cheap, too easy, too ready-made, too prefabricated. He chose to call the experience behind the church his "Hamlet moment," when he had everything, but that in having everything, he was reminded he had so little left.

In the months following the encounter behind the church, he developed a new thought path, similar to the faith first found in Hurricane Sandy, but this time much deeper, more fanciful, best expressed as a lecture in anthropology. This lesson was mostly narrated in dream time:

"Man was born in Africa roughly 50,000 years ago, the genetic record confirms." He felt this dream in narrative form, as if he were watching a PBS documentary on the journey of men. . . .

"Small bands of humans then walked to Australia, where the Ice Age froze them into huddles. They huddled tight for eons, sharing skins, but they then were forced across the seas of Indonesia by foot." "The fossil records show," Varlissima notes at this point in the dream, her voice sharper than usual, "that women were critical to this trespass. It was trespass," she insists, "but it was necessary to become who we are!"

At this point in the tale, he began to see the story of Adam and Eve as a primary evolutionary tale, more about natural history than actual biblical history.

"Men and women then decided that some of the family should split off—with a few settling in Central Asia and others in what became known as Europa."

"This must have been a painful set of decisions," Varlissima adds.

"Perhaps this was caused more by catastrophe than rational decision," he says, pulling her head closer to his.

The record does not yet fully explain this. There is a long pause for a dream interruption. Scientists scramble in the dream without answer. While a few others proceeded, most settled in Asia and Europe. How could this even have happened? When you study the rigor of the fossil record, it is nothing short of magical, this dispersion of man.

Then the most astonishing part of the tale began. . . .

The fossil record now claims that perhaps as few as five men and a dozen women, this small extended family cluster, walked across the Bering Strait into a new world of corn and sun and canyons." This dream was multi-layered. It allowed them both to feel certain, as a shiver was sent up their spines, that Varlissima and Colette would have been among these original women of trespass, preparing the new warriors.

It did not matter if he made that grade. He was blessed by having the thought about the key role of these women. What mattered was that Colette and Varlissima were there, with him now, capable of bringing new life into the mix of his mind, despite its harsh climate. This is the long view of the journey, the journey where survival itself is the surprise.

Races mix, eons pass, many go missing; in the end, some continue and survive. After so much pleasure, there was even more room for trespass. After this elaborate dream, what mattered was to step behind social sophistication—and to keep walking, as a species—in order to descend deeper than the presumed supremacy of the rational. This is what he thought about in that African mask in his front office.

His African mask was as bold as a Greek myth, full of these complex imperatives on how to live. It gave him a license to accept his aging, to no longer feel the need to hold the entire family upon his shoulders. *Succession was beginning to matter as much as self-definition.* This mask became a product of ultimate realism, showing him a world full of evil, unpredictable storms, rising waters, difficult friendships, dignity incarnate, and inevitable death and defeat. In contrast to this mask, it was modern religion that had become unrealistic, with its expectations of certain and earned salvation, and its simplification of wrong.

This mask helped him describe his mortal life as it really was—that is, fragile, threatened, uncertain, never consistently happy, and full of surprise. The three of them forged ahead, survivors—Colette, Varlissima, Bruce.

WHAT HE FOUND NEXT

HIRING THE BEST AT THE OLD STONE CHURCH OFFICE COMPLEX, 2000 to 2014

HE WAS NOW NEARING FIFTY-EIGHT. His firm was solid, growing, margins of profit looking as good as those of a start-up, but mature. But his body of energy was waning. Varlissima sized that up each night.

To his shock, Varlissima surprised him again, knowing what was building in him. For the simple realization that Varlissima had been his lover and wife for over half of his life took hold of his imagination, and she could see that would happen. She flirted with his thought path one night, joking that Dante never really had his muse Beatrice near. "That's what made her a special muse, right? . . . But here, we've been a couple for most of our adult lives." "What did this mean?" she jived, "Did it mean you really liked me?" Here her use of the past tense was deliberate, tense.

That next day he returned to work, to look over in detail what he had built. Was there an answer in his self-designed offices? He had designed his life to be about books and about people, but Varlissima was bringing up another topic: Is it possible to select ways to add missing people to your life and to your work?

It was true, his offices had more books than people, plenty more books. He could have grown his headquarters staff much larger, but he chose not to, populating growth through satellite offices and alliance partners in California and London and

Africa. He lived so much in the past, that perhaps Varlissima had a strong point here. He did not like too many people near, just the right ones.

He wondered the next week, after scanning a number of biographies by Jay Parini, if all writers who had finished at least ten books have this great advantage—stability at home, and stimulus to boot from lovers of active mind? Do they need empty offices, grand but austere? Do they want space from these lovers daily or monthly, or only in the long afternoons of self-reflection? Perhaps the reverse is mostly true: perhaps these muses need to squeeze productivity out of the writer's hippocampus with the pressure of many folks surrounding them. Perhaps a muse is only a muse when surrounded by the subject's friends and family? He began to reread the Greek myths. They were populous, and often hinged on a new person. He concluded the right mix of action and reflection was different for each writer, or perhaps for each book project!

He was getting somewhere in contemplating Varlissima again. He saw the opening she had made in his line of inquiry. Once again, they were speaking shorthand about their relationship and its survival.

What he found in obeying Varlissima's suggestion to bring more people into their lives proved bigger—bigger even than his respect for literary history. Part of the answer was to keep in mind family history, the Sicilian way.

Varlissima had grown up as the middle child in a family of five—"the perfect middle child," one of his Chinese friends noted. She always joked that she wanted "a home of chaos," constant visitors, kids galore, fun out of hand, and a ceaseless churning of birthdays, special events, family matters. Reading the biographies, he sensed some writers, like a Dickens or Márquez, thrived on these "families of chaos." But he and Varlissima had produced only one daughter.

This allowed a huge space to be filled by others in their lives. The gap was real, a psychic lacuna. And it was growing each month, as Colette prepared to enter her life away from home.

He paused to listen again to Varlissima's next phase of life suggestion, making sure he had not misunderstood the shorthand. Her suggestion, it seemed, was for him to bring more women into his life. The stage door was wide open, the potential visitors vast. He got what he needed on the road, but now he had to bring more home for Varlissima and his small and diminishing clan. It was merely a few years before Colette would be off to college.

Varlissima wanted more action at home, so he brought it on.

Suddenly, he found a new woman in their lives; Darlene. This was not fully surprising. This was actually a frequent, almost seasonal event, since his way of life required muses. He had written his business books with female researchers. His focus groups for business included teams of both sexes; but somehow, it was the women who seemed closest at hand when the most important stuff was near to harvest. Still, in Darlene's case, a case of natural beauty and presence, she brought something more significant, and potentially more difficult.

In the beginning, Varlissima spoke of Darlene in a role like their maid Rose had assumed in the twenty-five years she had worked for them—at best a family ally, a friend with whom you could trust your family and possessions. They trusted her with their daughter, their home, their cars, their church, their assets. But from the start, they both knew this Darlene, a composite of other muses before her, would prove a woman of consequence in their lives. More intuitively, Varlissima suggested that this new visitor might prove more helpful to them by working in his company offices. That was a brilliant idea, like when he had hired Rachel from Chicago more than fifteen years earlier.

Darlene was of Native American decent—a Huron Indian who loved Sugarland and the Dixie Chicks, and just about everything that sang with a harmony. She was the opposite of all those slow-talking intellectual heavyweights in his life now, and this is what made her wrongness right. The long valley of middle age was beginning to look predicable until Darlene arrived. She was so alive "she'd giggle at your funeral Bruce," one of his friends and webmaster, Frank Weaver, lamented, "while others might weep." Frank lived for James Joyce, and he was stunned when he found Darlene had never heard of him. Her respect for literary traditions was skin deep, her surface banter fun; she lived a life full of abandon.

What astonished him was Varlissima's encouragement of Darlene into their backyard. One summer, Darlene fulfilled with contractors Varlissima's design of a butterfly garden. The backyard went from three butterfly species to over two dozen winged angels each summer. Another summer, Darlene took him around to make the deals to build another corporate building, including "a meditation room designed to have the beast Bruce live longer than expected."

Most importantly, Varlissima saw that Darlene was like the return of his mother. Varlissima had crafted many quotable letters and zingers in her day, mostly to family. This from a long, incomplete letter to her older sister, Gale, in Seattle, that he had inadvertently found one bright spring day: "We could hear the magic of Lillian again in the friendly chatter and irreverent asides from Darlene," Varlissima wrote, expressing then how much they all missed Lillian in their lives.

Varlissima continued in her refined script:

In the primal way she speaks with incredible spirit and surprise about the smallest of things, Darlene "is" Lillian. Aunt Anne used to talk about her Eastern European ancestor returning as spring or summer butterflies. Darlene is no different, Gale. She will take the calls Bruce does not want to take, and win us favorable results with contractors and visiting friends. She is that instinctive. That protective of Bruce, even though he does not deserve it! She is exactly what he needs to keep his business and his writing afloat. Thank God she is around to pick up some of the slack from me, Gale.

In her outrageous jokes, in her sudden bursts of freedom, in her refusal to view him as her boss, Darlene was Lillian. Suddenly his place of work became the Yaddo of yesteryear, that special award-winning artist retreat in Saratoga, a place of creation and stillness, surprise and goals. He had everything again.

Even the people in his offices accepted Darlene, even though most found it a bit odd that someone the boss had known for a decade was now cleaning their bathrooms, and their rugs, and their desktops; arranging their folders when out of control; keeping it all feeling fun at work. She was too distracting to have around every day, so collectively, they decided to offer her part-time work, three half days. That proved splendid for all.

After so much war and startling loss in his early youth, Darlene was offering to him—both his home and his firm—a simple, different thing in their growing narrative: "If only you'd stop trying to be happy, you'd have a pretty good time of it."

MEETING DARLENE

FORT TICONDEROGA, NY

THERE WAS NOTHING INTELLECTUAL, NOTHING SEXUAL, in the appearance of Darlene in their lives. Instead, it was about the sensual, and the primal. Everyone in his life who met Darlene—lawyers, bankers, alliance partners, friends—felt her magic in different ways. She never finished college, but she gave advanced lessons to many.

Things had come full circle, in a sense. In youth, we are allowed to surround ourselves with stimulating folks from teammates to early lovers. But as we age, these people become dramatically more constrained by the conventions of marriage and family.

But occasionally, something magical and different happens. Darlene was liked by Varlissima and Colette, not just on Facebook, but deeply, very deeply. They enjoyed her. They trusted her. Darlene, they knew, was special to him in a primal way. In a parallel universe, Jay was important to him for inspiration. It was Darlene who jump-started new business ventures. At times, she would prove essential to his family. She knew something about his soul. She knew a great deal about his family and his history. She was a great listener who paid attention. She knew how to protect the pride. Slovak families often had special ladies hang around like this in the deeper past.

He knew many would misunderstand the role of Darlene in their lives. This was America, after all, a world far from Uncle Zigmund and Hurricane Sandy. Yet he also knew his life would improve with her in their space.

She could speak with him in a fashion more frank and more forceful than any. He had a strong ego that repelled criticism, but she had a new way to enter and twist his inner self. He often wrote his best stuff, his most creative passages, after a short whimsical exchange with her.

She always came up with zingers that he'd find surprising and fun to think through. Once, after spending three hours filing literary and corporate documents with him in the back office, she suddenly said, "Do not corner me, Bruce."

He had been working with her for hours, rather passively, in the corner of that back office, comfortably, pleasantly, so the comment was so primal, so out of the blue, that it was hilarious. He laughed out loud. People in other offices down the hall must have wondered what might be going on. But there was nothing happening but the strange space between her mind and his. Lillian had had the same effect on his creativity in youth, often saying outrageous things during a visit like "Bruce, give me some room, otherwise LP go home!" She said it with that same eerie sound of "ET go home!" As with his mom, this relationship with Darlene was built on forgiveness and calm, and often outrage.

He began to think through the moment of sudden rightness when he decided to let her into his inner circle, not just as a friend, not just as a worker, but as a soul helping to manage the inner sanctum of his ever-widening circle of friends and colleagues. Rasputin might have been a man turned female to come back as Darlene. No, he cautioned, it wasn't like that, she had no interest in any grab for power. She was just having fun.

He often wanted Darlene's secret assessment of a deal—even if he already had a few lawyers and key proven consultants in on the talks. She always saw something they had collectively missed about the essence of the visitors.

They sealed their deal while going to a fundraiser at Fort Ticonderoga. The year was 2012. Colette wasn't yet sixteen. There they sat, in the same place where 400 years before, Samuel de Champlain and the Huron fathers had signed their peace agreement, which lasted through the Revolutionary War. They agreed on the ride back to Saratoga that "they would work together for life, as they and their families aged." A very strange compact indeed. In the process, Colette came to understand how her father needed muses, not mistresses.

He now had three outstanding women in his life.

ADDING VERMONT STONES TO STONE CHURCH ROAD

REGRESSION INTO HISTORY AND INTO VERMONT

THERE IS NOTHING PRIVATE ABOUT WOMEN SUCH AS DARLENE: that is the secret as to why they prove consequential among families and friends and employees. They operate with little remorse and little repression, and they cause little regret. They are who they are, in any setting. They are like the earth—forgiving and forgetful.

He especially enjoyed the times that he, Darlene, and Colette went to Vermont to purchase quarry stones to build his meditation room out back, behind the group offices and headquarters. There was something permanent in his memory about those trips. Youth and Darlene would need to approve the pick of the purplish streaks in these quirky and cheap Vermont quarries, and he'd bring them the ninety miles home, despite the added transport costs. He was still frugal, but preparing to design for permanence.

Darlene dared him to think about his rushed life—and to rest from the endless ambitious narratives that swirled through his mind. "Do what really matters now, do not do everything," she warned. If Varlissima was the source of his wealth and his intellectual drive, then Darlene was the clean water mountain quenching his new thirst for balance and wellness.

Women with many tongues speak the languages of loyalty, alertness, conditioning, playtime, adaptability, harm and failure, trespass, and returning home. Most important, their tips about life and happiness add up. Darlene said, "The only thing that works in old age is a brave face, a good tailor, weekly massages, comfortable shoes, and joy." She also insisted that "old age is always twenty years older than I am."

WOMAN WITH MANY TONGUES

FROM LUSAKA, ZAMBIA,
TO THE FRENCH AND INDIAN WARS

HIS MANAGEMENT FIRM now had complex teams working on food security in Africa, and several larger contracts serving the global firms that brought oil and gas to a world of 7 billion souls. He even ran a high-end, multi-year benchmarking workshop on innovation, carbon threats, and energy trends, including fifteen of the largest firms in the world.

The more he spoke with Darlene, weighed in with Colette, and discussed even his least-productive ideas with Varlissima, the less he needed the expense of some of his contract attorneys. He also needed less time in the office, as his back office was mighty and strong, and again run by women more organized and more deliberate than he could ever prove to be. He began to feel that these women spoke with many tongues, and that their differences made his competitiveness more sensible.

Yet the larger his practice became, the more he found comfort in smaller, distinct, non-intellectual items, such as that statue of the deer whose antlers could hold candles. He would come to call this "the Darlene Effect." Perhaps this was the ultimate end zone of training he got from a lifetime of reading the classics.

He had placed this bronze artifact on the fireplace mantel in honor of the poet Wallace Stevens, who had written "Anecdote of the Jar," one of his favorite simple poems. Like the deer in his office, that jar, which had been placed upon a hill in Tennessee, held dominion over everything. When Darlene was not around, he felt his deer a fine and appropriate substitute for her good cheer. When she was around, he admired the deer's pride and silence over him. Darlene dusting the deer was one of his favorite mo-ments in a business week. It was all odd, and wonderful.

A treasure trove surrounded this deer, adding grandeur to his ever-mounting collection of books. He loved reading regional history now, however detailed, between business calls. He would reread books like *Bloody Mohawk: The French and Indian War and the American Revolution.*

Stories about the role of Fort Ticonderoga four hundred years earlier hounded him—it was one of the few surrounding constants in the area, besides the Hudson River and the Adirondacks themselves. His need to feel up close the spirit of longevity was beginning to unnerve him, except in his visits to Japan and Europe, where the buildings spoke to him. He could now see Samuel de Champlain signing the papers with the Huron. He could see himself there. He knew that this vision was telling him something about his future.

It all clicked one day. He had bought the Bentley estate, which had been built around 1760, to bring it into his family's future. He thought about its succession of owners—the seven generations of Bentleys—the way they gathered the fieldstones to build the church across the road in 1824, the way Doctor Hunt bought it from the Bentleys during the Great Depression, and in extending it, readied it for his purchase.

The entire history clicked one day. He must stop roaming the world, and invest in his homestead. He must make his writing and his home matter. He could feel succession now in his bones. He cultivated the feeling more and more.

CHOOSING THE RIGHT POND

HIS LIBRARY GROWS

ONE OF THE BEST BOOKS he'd never read was *Choosing the Right Pond,* by Robert Frank, a professor of economics at Cornell. He brought this book at least a dozen times on his Caneel Bay vacations in the Virgin Islands, but never found the time read it. Manta rays and schools of fish were what filled those days. He would mail the book to Room 13 at this former Rockefeller resort, but never opened it. By the tenth visit, he just mailed it out of ritual.

As he turned fifty-nine, he read much into that title. This concept of choosing the right pond helped him escape some of the remorse that surrounded him during the first half of his middle age, and through most of the depression he felt in youth. How could that happen? Well, it allowed him to become more social and far less internal. It was about the right pond, not him. It was about business, and the business of books, nothing more. It was wrong to think too much about the vastness of the ocean; it was more important to choose the right pond. Life was about smart choices. Granted, places like Amsterdam, New Orleans, Colette's Paris, Fellini's Rome and Rimini, and Istanbul had more to offer than Saratoga—but then again, they offered too much.

Freedom was about choosing the right size for his options. After choosing Saratoga as his pond, he found himself standing alone in his yard one day and thinking, *"How perfectly silly it is to discount the wondrous."*

He kept an image of Caneel Bay, with two boats and a dock, in his mind even in winter when at home. This new-found ability to ignore the experts, to forget about the return in the equation, to sidestep complexity that will not yield, offered a kind of protection that was deeper than his middle-aged remorse. He was, in a sense, becoming priceless.

He no longer needed to understand Shakespeare if the people around him made him feel Shakespearean. Darlene had finally read *Doing More With Less,* and she found it "funny." In being able to laugh with Darlene, he had become freer and in the right pond.

After many a business trip or speaking engagement, he would sit near the pond across from the Old Stone Church, chomping on a Churchill cigar and eyeing his blooming flowerbeds. He really hated TV, really liked radio, but liked the interaction of large groups even more. Sometimes Darlene or Varlissima or Colette would join him during these peaceful garden visits. This family bliss was beyond his normal fears of middle age.

Watching these moments of sudden rightness increased in frequency as he neared sixty. Was this the simple decline in aging, a mental shift that happens to all as the testosterone levels wane? His vision of missing persons became more stimulated. He had crossed into a state of play where they were him, and he was them. He came to recognize a set of higher facts that he wanted to pass along to future generations: "Hey youth! Watch out! You can piss away your youth trying to decide which ocean to jump into and when. But you can become quite anxious at the beach, doing nothing. You must choose the right pond."

He saw that in choosing the *right* pond, he had entered the near perfect future. He described this state to Varlissima one night, and she said: "You always get this way when finishing a book." "What way?" he asked. "All warm and fuzzy and mystical." He felt as if he had broken a code that mattered now, since he brought those same feelings away from book writing into his life. It was in the tone of things now—in the wind by his home, not the leaves whirling in the wind. The atmosphere at the Old Stone Church felt like a crossing.

Then one day everything changed again.

He calculated the anticipated values of his eight TIAA-CREF retirement accounts, tabulated the worth of his firm if projected with modesty, added the value of his home and its related and unrelated property, and decided, "Shit, I can become a pensioner." And he did.

He decided that he would spend a quarter of his time consulting, run his staff a quarter of the time, and write during the other half of his lifetime. He talked this over with his three women. Varlissima said, "About time." Colette said, "That'd be supreme, Dad." And Darlene said, "Why not?" He took the dive.

To celebrate the decision, Varlissima planned a surprise trip to the beaches on Long Island where he was born. To mock his belly, Darlene bought him a Buddha for the garden. "Semi-retirement," she said, "will make you huge, Bruce!" Varlissima thought it a mean trick, a mean gift, this mockery of his rather large, rotund belly. *He kept the white Buddha there for decades, outliving most of his friends.* He felt at last that he understood the power in a compassionate Buddha.

A MOTHER'S DEATH
CONTEMPLATING NEW FORMS OF FREEDOM
2010 to 2014

IN THIS LARGER, MORE EXPANSIVE SETTING, where he would romp and enjoy circumstances even at home, even while in his home offices, his mother's death proved priceless. She had been dead four years now, but she was still teaching him, shaping him.

As he matured at work, winning the attention of staffs from Europe to Africa and Australia, his mother's death somehow made more space in his heart for Varlissima, for Darlene, and for Colette. This was almost the opposite of what he saw in many of his business mates. He had always loved his mother, but now that she was missing, he found that he loved the remaining women in his life even more.

And this is precisely why it made the ordinary elements in his life extraordinary. It seemed odd, but the more time he invested with these women, the greater the impact and profit of his work teams. He wondered why it took three decades for him to discover this about team success.

He attributed his good luck to how he had been raised by his mother. Once he had learned how best to invest in memory, the death of his mother extended his wings in a manner larger than commonsense.

He came to believe that, as promised, Lillian was keeping it all tied together up there for them—so they would not, could not, fail. She had given him the logic of remorse. The logic of remorse is hard to explain, especially to men, but it proves priceless in its consequences. Remorse proves liberating. He could say to his lover, "I must get to work. Sorry, but I miss you already." He could say to a business partner, "Sorry, I must leave for vacation— my daughter is waiting, but I miss you already." He'd say to himself, *"I have bigger things before me."*

Miraculously, he had to admit he had become one of the lucky ones.

A FATHER'S DEATH

MEMORIES FROM PICTURES,
FEELINGS FROM AFAR

HE WOULD NEVER FINISH this thought path because he had so little to go on. For decades, he had blamed everyone he knew for his father's death. Having been raised by his grandmother, mother, and sister, he had to invent his masculinity—from muscle and bone to making his place in a world of markets.

His father would break his long silence only on rare occasions. In this way, Walter was the opposite of his mother, who could return on a dime. He found this not sad, but odd.

In his World War II pictures, Walter was tall, thin, and quiet looking, and he also looked reserved—not meant to be in this world very long. Walter had never really spoken to him as a parent, so Bruce had no real direct recollection of the sound of his father's voice, or the look on his face when he held him as a child—so all of this needed, wanted, to be reconstructed by the higher winds of memory.

In one faded photo, Walt—with cigarette in hand, hanging around a rock in Hawaii during his days serving in the Pacific— looked much like George Blair, before he became known to the world as George Orwell.

He had been Walter's child for such a short time—less than three years, two months, and a few long summer days. Yet Walt returned to him on occasion, especially when he was under stress.

WE FLOWER UNDER STRESS

REMEMBERING A BASEMENT ON LONG ISLAND, FORTY-FIVE YEARS LATER, 2014

IN THE MIDDLE OF THE NIGHT, he had one of his feverish thought paths. He was edging sixty. He knew that many modern men either retired or died within a decade or two of that signal age. He had already consumed a half-century and more in finding his place. His father had left at thirty-nine, and he had cousins who checked out in their forties. This mathematical urgency began to run beside his days.

This led to his next big thought in reshuffling his life: he should not stop, as he always flowered under stress. He sought stress. Without it, he might cease. The next night's dream was intense. He felt the dream in the third person, as if his mother was lecturing him about the actions he was taking, but at the same time, understanding those actions for the first time . . .

You are with Sally in her basement; her mother's washing machine is making noise above the groans, as her father, who is also the school principal, is cutting the lawn.

You can see him from the basement window mowing lane by lane, moving farther away from you as you stand against the wall with the tight body of Sally nearby. You experience the stress. You press her groin against that wall, and rub, and she wants that, knowing that in minutes her father will be too far away from the basement wall to be able to look in easily at two fifteen-year olds.

But as long as her father's angle of receding takes him away from the angle of seeing you, she wants more.

As the stress mounts, you know he can bend over at any second into discovery, and you know he will come back near you and peer in soon enough. At the same time, you can feel the moisture in her pants, and you know that you will always—somehow—flower under stress.

This is the stress of success.

Like big Dutch tulip bulbs, we pop up from the earth in the shadow of our parents, and while they give us the food and shelter of early growth, they also help us flower by leaving.

Life is simply too large, too lusty, too loving to stop this pursuit of stress and joy, profit and pleasure.

The dream ends. . . . To try to make sense of it, he recalls a passage from Walt Whitman's *Leaves of Grass* in which he notes:

> *Youth, large, lusty, loving—*
> *youth full of grace, force, fascination.*
> *Do you know that Old Age may come after you*
> *with equal grace, force, fascination?*

He had loved that passage throughout his life.

So often, an experience in his life had come full circle. What started as a nightmare, a fear, had become a poetic lesson, a vignette of memory that recites an essence, a meaning, and a hope.

FRANKLY TORN

AT HOME

BY NOW, MANY WERE ASKING how a poor boy had made millions, had roamed into so many distinct multinationals.

He loved the questions; he felt good about the attention. Yet he was frankly torn about how to respond. Could he answer with the same boldness about the thousands of business leaders he had met to make himself? Or was there something particularly perverse about that thought? He was frankly torn by these questions, yet they kept coming at him, and each new book he published only increased their rate of attack.

This was a part of his eccentric good luck: people turned to him to help him, and he accepted the attention. He attributed his knowledge of teamwork to all his years as a street basketball player. And perhaps the maturing of his organizations could be attributed to this higher fact: he strove in everything he did to remain coachable. There was always a way to improve, to be taught a new move, so many hung near to give him advice, most of which he found a way to use, thankfully.

What drew him to business was the complexity, the energy of it, the relationships. Across three decades, his guests enjoyed fun and cheer and learning at the same time, and paid big bucks for the chance. He imagined these workshops vividly beforehand, planning them to a T with his staff, and he came to think that there was something classic in assembling them. It was not so much a party of leaders as a team of leaders, and not so much a gathering across many regions as a sanctuary he had made.

Okay, he was one of the lucky ones. Success was not about self-help, after all. It was about helping many others: gradually, a reputation for helping many rose around him and his teams.

The life of business proved to be fun.

FREEDOM AND FATE AND WILLIAM HOGARTH

MANCHESTER ENGLAND, 2010

IN SOME OF HIS BUSINESS BOOKS, he tried to define leadership as the balance of panic and resolve, the balance of personal freedom with the acceptance of fate. But as enrollment in his workshops kept growing, he came to conclude that "leaders like to learn from leaders." That was where the magic resided.

While working in England, he decided to visit some museums to see if he could find any works of art that captured the essence of business. William Hogarth, whose work appears in several British museums, first answered his search. Hogarth's paintings proved extraordinary; in them he found an array of folks, all interacting, all in a sense needing each other.

Hogarth had depicted the world in much the same way Bruce saw business. Always about street life—people who were wobbly on their feet, or those already horizontal and asking for a loan. It wasn't noble literary or professional aspirations that formed the essence of business, the meat of business. Sure, his life was full of lawyers, accountants, vendors, and subcontractors—but they were like him, motivated by the same desires. He saw all this in Hogarth's work.

There is a background story connected with the painting above. Hogarth had gone with some friends for a little merrymaking in London's Highgate section. Along the way, they were diverted inside a public house. Before long—was it the warm beer? was it the smiling ladies in yellow?—one of the younger men struck another on the head with a quart pot, cutting him severely. Well, to make a long legend longer: as the blood streamed down the man's face, Hogarth picked up a pencil and began sketching the scene, with both stunning realism and a sense of sportiveness.

Like him, Hogarth was interested in bonding—in how people do business together. It wasn't about the nine to five. It was about full body contact, about days of jest and jovial pursuits, as well as profit. In a single day, he'd often confer or talk with at least sixty different people from dozens of locations, often working in teams of four to six on the phone at once. He liked the constant party, and would experience a lot in a little.

Hogarth, without ever muttering a word, taught him a great deal about his good fortune and about his nature, too. He reminded Bruce that life was a feast.

ALL ICE IS DANGEROUS

A FROZEN RIVER NEAR HAMILTON STREET
POTSDAM, NY, 1982

CLOSE TO MIDNIGHT ONE WINTER NIGHT, he had seen a bike rider circling on the frozen Raquette River in Potsdam, New York. During the frigid winters, the surface of the Raquette, which courses through the town, would freeze and remain solid for several months.

This long-distant memory froze in his mind for decades. He could not outpace it, for it was connected with a tragedy. That same winter, a fellow Clarkson professor—one with whom he and Varlissima had shared a rented triplex—had died beneath that same ice in a terrible accident. It was a devastating event that left his colleague's young children without a father. Being fatherless himself, Bruce felt a painful connection with the tragedy on many levels.

So in his memory, the haunting image of this lone bike rider was both good and bad, both liberating and utterly depressing. This faceless person, who rode in circles on the frozen river, had shown him that life could remain magically open for trying most anything, while others sunk beneath the ice. He realized he had become like that bike rider: skidding on the ice of business, riding with joy into the literary. And again, like the night rider, he recognized his balance was mostly luck, as others fell beneath the same ice. People thought of him as a decent professor at Clarkson. He thought of himself as a writer and businessman. It was this shifting set of differences that wore thin with time, so he had to move to survive. His success wasn't based at all on courage, but simply on the art of remaining balanced and open, like the survivor on ice.

Much of his life had become a balancing act to stay erect as he bumped into things and people each day. This balancing took the daily disciplines he knew from his basketball days. He took many spins, tried many teams, ran after many gigs. He was no professor in retrospect. He was a boy, curious in action. He wrote a motto to act by: "Actors speak of imaginary things as if they are real. Academics speak of real things as if they are imaginary."

Yes, all ice remained dangerous.

All ice is dangerous, but that is what gave his life its beauty and its stark brilliance. What enabled his survival remained the mystery.

VENTURE UNDERSTANDING

ACCEPTING RISK,
SIFTING THROUGH WHAT MATTERS

HE FOUND VISUALIZING THE NEAR FUTURE a useful weapon. It helped him mature and sift through what really mattered. He could now dismiss most requests almost instantly— for example, he never financed extensive risk evaluations, nor did he pay much for legal advice. Instead, he executed fast on what mattered most.

He began to look at dangers in business. It was wonderful to be able to analyze and think through risks. It reminded him often of pivots, of moves on the basketball court from his youth. Danger was beautiful to him. It was several lovely young women inviting him into the lily pond next door.

He thought of the market in which he worked as a pond. Survival in that pond, where it was easy to drown, was about the teams, not about the terms. It was about the pond, not the profit. It was never really about him. That is what he loved the most about business. He was often the one to jump into the pond first and take its temperature before others would harvest the lilies. For him, it was all about preparing for the muddy moments when the road gets dark—so, if necessary, he could throw the spark. He judged his team by secret measures like trust. This wasn't so much talent collection, as talent liberation.

He did his time with discipline—always asking himself before the dive in, "What can we get done, and what must we leave undone?" This made him pursue a select life. Most in business called this an exit strategy. He considered it always an entrance strategy, a channel to something more magical and more mysterious, namely relationships and friendships, agreements in action.

He had a feminine attitude towards business. He would win when others in the pond won, not before. This proved to be the way he got them into his pond.

REGRESSION IS PROGRESSION

OLD STONE CHURCH OFFICES, DURING A COLD FEBRUARY

THOSE WHO HE THOUGHT WERE MISSING were not, in the end, missing after all. He would descend into the pond with them in mind, and slowly embrace each along the way. They proved soul mates, and loving partners. They all resided where we store the affection in our brains, a spark beneath surface attitudes. Regression proved progression, in his case.

He reasoned out loud, *"If anger and fear and surprise make this world dominated by event, not thought, why not start again in action, beyond blame?"*

He was slowing down deliberately. This idea of selection proved special to him, like the number of shots required to net thirty points in forty-eight minutes; this way he might survive the flooding of blame, the floating totems, the many things spinning in muck with sharp teeth and claws and needs that some describe as a market.

And hell—if he failed, if he got stuck, the muck and dive were worth it from the start. Not entirely entering the pond was the mistake in life. It was all about intelligent optionality, as they say in big oil.

All it took was a sense of humor, a love of most people, and a willingness to risk and to fail. In this sense, his business life was exactly like a basketball finals game, except the rewards were more tangible. They were always more about freedom than profit. Business was full of beginnings, his African mask reminded him daily.

Beginning in his youth, and throughout his middle years, blame was thrown at him. Guilt was when he caught blame and began juggling it, with wit and calm. Remorse was the lovely flight away that kept him free. He came to understand how much faster he could be than blame—that anchor, that ugly host, who was the ugly umpire of most lives.

He concluded: the more you climb the ladder, the more the world can see the monkey's ass. *"If youth is large and lusty, then middle age might prove immense and worthy."* He insisted on telling himself this again and again, like a mesmerizing mantra. It was his strongest thought after the birth of Colette.

What mattered was that the youthful man had become a husband, the writer a disciplined craftsman, the traveler a student of different ways. What no longer mattered was just as significant. Fate was kinder to him. Stinkbugs no longer fell into his coffee each morning: the assassin bugs stayed on the other side of his office windows, looking in; but he was now beyond their touch.

THE SECOND OBSESSION

THE ENDLESS LOCATIONS OF
BEING IN BUSINESS, THE GAME ITSELF

THE SECOND OBSESSION, LIKE THE FIRST, had a reflective quality. He was always aware of performing. This made every conversation he found himself in a performance—where jobs derived from a random airport flight, and staffers arrived from very funny and public exchanges that proved of great consequence. He was on, they said, all day long.

He once hired one of his most profitable young staffers after spotting her on a bicycle outside his post office. Just like that, he decided to walk over to this stranger and start a conversation, telling her about the CEO he had just called. After a bit of back-and-forth banter, intuitively, he offered her a job. She was impressed, moved to his town, and doubled in value to the firm each year for the six years before she left for Goldman Sachs. She had no initial expertise in his field; but he was certain, in an instant, she'd work out simply from that initial conversation outside the post office. He did this "risk hiring" again and again as his firm grew. Sometimes it was a disaster, most of the time it worked. There was no need for technical expertise; he could train that. He didn't have so much a business plan as a long-term social exposure plan. He meant to remain in the game.

He guessed he glued onto this behavior first on the basketball court, where the great scouts were hidden in all audiences. You must be a jokester, you must be a jester to gain attention. Sometimes during an interview to hire, he'd do the business equivalent of Michael Jordan's double-pump fade away, and it would be a swoosh. Letting them know too much fails. You must be sportive in your seriousness. Born with a love of reading, he cultivated a certain forcefulness in business settings, a penchant for leaning into his future with wit, a boy on the loose. Work had to be fun, as well as fundamental.

Ben Franklin had taught him to be frugal, inventive, and whenever humor allowed, diplomatic. This was the primary path to accepting grace. But there was also this direct wit that won folks over to his wants. It wasn't so much manipulation as his fascination *in them* that allowed his needs to emerge and be satisfied.

He found himself a businessman, without ever formally studying business. He had never taken a single formal business class in his life! Yet, in the 1990s, he found himself a professor of business because he had founded a firm, and deans of business admired his books and teaching style.

When he would win some, others would most likely lose some. He would win more, and others would lose more. Before he knew it, he was compounding value to his firm with less and less effort, miles above actual earnings of his particular day. For when you are the founder, there is little significance in per diem.

For years, he could not comprehend a fire without first staring at its bright kernel, obsessively, like a dog at camp's edge, determining how to add more logs to the risk until it was ripe for his intervention, as the others left the ring of heat. He sought out the situations where he could outlast, out-prepare those around him, like in a basketball finals tournament—and be the first to pick through the ashes for gems.

He never was high enough in the organizations he advised to lose his head when failure surrounded his clients. He often felt like a jester at court, who could be ignored during the rush for accountability.

Varlissima didn't need to know the details, another beauty in having a smart Sicilian as a lifelong wife. She had no patience for the complexities of currencies, earnings, and taxes overseas. But he showed Colette the paper notes with a kind of fatherly glee.

Here was the queen who graced the front of the Canadian dollar, her expression happier and less stern than the image on the British pound. Here was the South African twenty-rand note, with a smiling Nelson Mandela on one side, elephants emerging from the other, and prehistoric hunters pursuing gazelles on the security screen. Here were the crisp notes from his clients around the world. He now kept them in small boxes to view and share.

In a sense, liberating the creative rather than the professional side of himself allowed him to change the work–play balance. Relationships, respect, and then revenue: the mantra defined his life.

VARLISSIMA IN WONDERLAND
BACK IN MEMORY, TOUCHING HIS WIFE
AFTER PROFIT, 2014

ALICE, DEAR, IMAGINE MY VARLISSMA. She is like you, living in dread of aristocracy. Imagine why she traded all her early advantages for "this little Polish Marine butt," whom she dragged into becoming a world traveler after having fallen down a dark hole with him. This female in proper British male clothing runs alongside him like an imaginary friend. When they are alone at home, she is a lady squirrel without hesitation—swirling by his side like a pulsating Madonna.

Varlissima will not eat proper British meats, but she will eat him in this fantasy again and again—and like you, dear Alice, he grows back each night, when she eats him again, until seventeen years later they are wed.

Who is to say what is proper? Why should she not eat him, if that is her dream? What's sweet is the continual flourish that incites a rising sea between them. This makes the vanity of human wishes seem inconsequential.

The halo grows each time he sticks into her: it seals his bond to fly. "Jake," she says, "Make the bond." They scream at him, his stern advisors, until he and she fly off, banking left together.

"That's it." "Keep doing that." "That's it." They chant the same chant as they fly. "That's exactly it." They dream together in a white soft cocoon made by no machine—without clothes, unbothered by material cares, with their asses not yet slapped by the stern family of gods next door.

"The gods really don't care," she says, being that half of him that loved defiance. He likes when she says this.

"After all, they know what humans are like," he says, reassuring her. She makes her back loose, resting for more.

"That's why they put us in a box of rules in the first place," he suggests. They giggle, and proceed in this sweet ritual and routine. The cocoon softens further.

At the peak of their peak during the first days, he sees a sign on a door that says "No Poles, No blacks, No dogs"—as if the world had been stuck in 1942. But she accepts this Pole, finds his sticky ways worth it. He sticks with her, traveling her world, knowing more than ever why he should have been born female.

Her red hair stands up in the air after she eats him, as if the earth had flipped exactly upside down.

He just allows her to be the female, never saying "Easy, girl!" and never saying, "You know I am riding you." She puts him on a taller horse. This causes more frequent spouts of temporary bliss, and her satiety is visible, and her sense of adventure satisfied, as she binds them again through feasting. They breathe hard together as they join insides. A strange caterpillar stamps the bottom of their naked feet one night with the same sign of approval. "Hell, we don't need society! We don't need a profession! Piss on tuition. We have ourselves."

They descend into the moist thickets of pleasure: she calls him the damp man. He likes that, having always been embarrassed before about how easily athletes sweat. More exciting threats appear—these muses have green eyes—but he chases them off one by one, enjoying the dismissal process. Varlissima's eyes open even wider. Her legs open even wider. Her mind opens even wider. He sees that the scalp of her pleasures fits his mind perfectly.

After what seems like a century, he finally kicks all the competitors away. This lifetime with the vested squirrel surrounds him totally—and suddenly, it seems like overnight now, she is no longer the girl whose hair stands tall near him. Her hair falls into place. The hole that invited them in invites them out.

She clips her locks—feigning disinterest in fashion; but like Samson, she appears more acceptable now before all charmers:

men, women, and girls. She emerges from the hole: transformed by her Pole, pleased by the company of strange creatures that helped her hop past ideology. She eyes the outside again (life is bright, welcoming again), and embraces those awfully unique experiences for years by never referring to them.

She starts feeling as if both of them are doubling in size and consequence each year in the outside world. They have now arrived in Saratoga, eyeing the Old Stone Church for purchase. She remembers the first time, as Eve, that she ate his apple, how that felt when the innocence was lost. She eats him again and again. She throws her head back in joy. She is controlling their destiny, and he likes her in this cave called their first home.

She tells no one for decades about this guy in her life: for the life of her, it is a sweet secret. She has a thousand nicknames for him at home, but only one in public—"partner." He is more pleased that they grow together in this half-underground cave; without much furniture, with no bright decorated vases; but with roots and vegetables they survive, with joy and closeness. They remain lean in their fascinations for years. The days are routine, businesslike. But it still seems chemical at night, luminous. As they race on, the world gives them the chance to grow in love.

It is a dream where nothing really bad happens, so she keeps eating. This makes the vanity of human wishes seem inconsequential, and on trial.

When Varlissima leaves this first underworld, nature itself has become brighter than the sun. She knows in her veins why the oceans will flood the world. Venturing a bit outside the cave, she learns the name of each bird; animals are her jewels, and she divides up Father Time as the original gods contemplated: one week each year with insects, a month with waxy plants, three months with British teas.

And then each night she eats him again, allowing his freedom and her swollen captivity another dance. His world of work is widening. He is now traveling for higher fees. He misses her each night that he is far away, but he remembers her touch as if was yesterday. Frida can have his fly—Varlissima has his soul.

She becomes a wife and a domesticated squirrel, organizing his and her maids; their children of the future increase as well, but they choose to live away from this fantasy. . . . The neighboring nymphs that clean up for them distract him some nights; they are so young, so still in his gaze, more like antelopes before a car than a squirrel in British attire. What an offense at first, this sensual set of realizations in the reality of middle age! But they remain quiet and true and solemn and good for each other into a fourth decade!

This lifetime with the vested squirrel near him—so near, like breath itself—has slowed and changed Varlissima. She is no longer the girl whose hair stands tall next to him. She is more responsible, despite her red hair.

As they awaken, they skip into a dark purpled older age.

AN AFTERLIFE
AT THE OLD STONE CHURCH

"YOU DO NOT NEED TO KNOW exactly what something is to know that it can be dangerous," he overheard Sigmund, his neighbor, assert once on a whim.

That afternoon, he was feeling profoundly the stern weight of aging. He had just finished three glorious hours in tight conversation with Darlene.

The sun was hot, he felt a bit relaxed. His heart stopped.

The clouds paused, but not for long, over Old Stone Church Road. For a few infinite minutes, no cars rushed by. No trucks passed. The baskets of bougainvillea swayed in the wind. He was mostly still. Suddenly, he felt a playful wiggle in his pants, as if memory itself were pure pleasure.

His second surprise was that his deepest and most accurate self—his writing self—could live on after his well-suited, well-heeled, but finite self had completely expired. Was this what his TIAA-CREF advisors had recommended that he and Varlissima plan for in his family legacy?

So much of his physical body had become a word body. His anger subsided. His aggressiveness subsided. He went from earning to royalties. His needs did a little Irish dance. Darlene helped him sit up. Sitting him up, he readjusted his fatigue, and sat down to rest like an old man during a St. Patrick's Day festival, beer in hand, but sipping nothingness.

On the second day of his afterlife, he saw and enjoyed many comical things. Insects began to matter much more, and the wind spoke to him. He was relieved to discover that the Zuni believe that the beautiful resides near the dangerous. He should have suspected that from his knowledge of Darlene, but he had been so busy with his first life, with the business of life itself, that he had missed this majestic point beneath it all.

Now he saw that everything is beautiful, and that most things are dangerous, but they coexist in a world of good and evil, in a playpen of men and women, in a time of glory and failure. He was deeply satisfied now, but did not know why. He did not need to make a choice between any longer.

He spoke to God as if he were talking to a friend, and for the first time in a long time, he liked everything he heard going on around him from the music to the chatter between speakers. Things, in general, became simple to handle. His normal daily impatience evaporated.

Three days later he reemerged in public.

Perhaps this quiet plentitude explains why the Zuni cluttered their altars with Katchina dolls, Christian artifacts, and the heads of bears; why Frida cluttered her paintings with monkeys, interwoven strains of vegetation, and necklaces of thorns. Darlene, too, had cluttered her days with shining things, from toe rings to elaborate earrings, with oils and ancient incense made from Biblical nectars. This, he decided, would be his new way of being—a mixing and a matching, not a selective set of the finer things, but a magical inclusion of all things.

Dying helped him get past the rough, wordless world that surrounded him with remorse. He could now see things as they were. Words became magical, the way they are in dreams. Simple events became the blueprints to the back alley. His memories could watch things become meaningful.

The questions he asked himself changed rapidly. "What do we do when bad things happen to good people?" became "What do we do when good things happen to bad people?"

After his own death, he realized that he had thought of himself as a bad person for having failed to awaken his father that morning so long ago. On the first day God created man; on the second he had a better thought.

Everything remained in his afterlife: the old house, the newly reframed offices, and the Old Stone Church itself. They still stood, but became more visible in a starker, more direct light. Varlissima lived on, of course, and so did the lovely Colette, maturing into a real beauty. The missing persons who had constructed his first self were now everywhere in his mind; they were his dwelling; they were with him constantly. But there was still more.

Varlissima got stronger when he first died.

Varlissima became more beautiful with age, and more surprising than his words about her. "Varlissima," he asked one day, "who are you looking for?" She stopped looking, accepting her fate. "Everything proves possible under God," Lillian had said in times like this.

She didn't know he could hear her in the other room, when he recited these discoveries. She was thunder feet running in the attic of his mind, and he could no longer strive to guide her, to walk with her. He just had to let her be.

She was exactly herself all along, it turned out.

He could never have stopped her flooding. Yet she had become fully the mother of Colette, a child of three centuries.

He had died. And she had risen.

PART THREE

AT OLD STONE CHURCH

"Eighty! I can hardly believe it. . . . My father, who lived to 94, often said that the 80s had been one of the most enjoyable decades of his life. He felt, as I begin to feel, not a shrinking but an enlargement of mental life and perspective. One has had a long experience of life, not only one's own life, but others', too. One has seen triumphs and tragedies, booms and busts, revolutions and wars, great achievements and deep ambiguities, too. . . . One is more conscious of transience and, perhaps, of beauty. . . . I do not think of old age as an ever grimmer time that one must somehow endure and make the best of, but as a time of leisure and freedom, freed from the factitious urgencies of earlier days, free to explore whatever I wish, and to bind the thoughts and feelings of a lifetime together. . . ."

—OLIVER SACKS
EXCERPT FROM "THE JOY OF AGING. (NO KIDDING.)"
THE NEW YORK TIMES, JULY 6, 2013

Prelude

The Magic in Old Age

OUR HOMES LIVE LONG AFTER US. As we age, our homes become our core, our deepest sense of self. They become a statement of our trust in the future, what we leave behind for our loved ones.

A home's revealing tone remains as basic and essential and as common as moisture to a plant. While memory is the succulent, the home remains the very structure of meaning in all the family narratives of friends, good fortune, and near misses. That is why so many believe in ghosts and spirits, who seek refuge in their familiar surroundings.

At this point in human history, there is a large amount of literature on the chemistry and biology of love and sex, but little about the science of our bodies and our families at home.

It is easier to study mating outside the home than nesting in the home. What mattered to Bruce now was the survival of his home, Reverend O.J. Bentley's pre-Revolutionary farm estate. For it was here, in itself, that his home enabled the growth in his family and friends.

Humans move about a lot more than plants, but they are like plants to the sun of their own memories. A good home absorbs those memories.

In housing our families properly, we experience something both ancient and modern. Homes house our longing and our remorse—things far more important, in the end, than cash or blame. These housed memories are succession manifest, our emotions written large on a canvas that lasts. Homes shape our children, and foster an answer to their fears.

Perhaps this is why many cultures call the nexus of land and property "an estate and a living trust." Of course, a trust is a specific legal instrument that allows an estate to bypass probate and pass directly to the individual selected. But the many cultures that see higher facts in this arrangement know it is about much more than tax relief. In this way, a text is very much like a home.

A text can bring us backward or forward with ease and grace and surprise, in a fashion swifter and more significant than logic. This way, works on his office shelves by the likes of Jonathan Edwards and Casanova and Gabriel García Márquez housed his imagination over time—and over horizons larger than a single generation. The world's most beautiful and exceptional books are like mansions.

A book, then, is a large, sustained interconnected statement of trust, a chosen display of our shared faith in a near future. Every book holds within a stern proposition: "Come into my home."

A DRUNKEN HERCULES

IT WAS NEVER TOO LATE to respect his neighbors as himself. During Colette's early years, his neighbors seemed as far away as Asia or Antarctica. But now that she had grown and he was spending less time traveling and more time working closer to home, he'd be a stubborn and forlorn fool if he did not get to know, and get known in, his neighborhood.

What he loved, what he found special, about neighbors was that they arrived at his same place, often by chance. There was no overarching single pattern to the discovery of his neighborhood—so different and so random when compared with the discovery of Colette.

His afternoon walks were like clockwork. He could feel his neighbors' eyes from behind their shaded window panes. But after many gestures of hello, only a few bolder neighbors would invite him in. Approximately 36.4 million World Cup watchers would tweet during the soccer games, but only a few neighbors could let him into their worlds.

He began to sense a magical spider web that was woven around his neighborhood. He could see how relationships beget reputations, and that reputations beget revenue. He would see the shimmering of this web on some nights, and in the twinkle of early mornings right beside the blue morning glories. He even saw it during the business day—if the glint of the light was just right, he felt it nearing, magical. In the house on Old Stone Church Road, a world emerged that he found intoxicating.

He recalled, as a young man, encountering the shocking statue of the drunken Hercules in the British Museum: a heavy wooden club rested on his left shoulder, and in his right hand he held his penis as he pissed into the House of Stags. His massive head was tilted in relief, his marble thighs spread wide.

This memory made him think of his own figure. Seeing himself in relief, on Old Stone Church Road, he began to see himself as other's saw him—like the drunken Hercules, ready to menace the House of Stags, yet distracted for all eternity by a deep urge. It was most lucky that his neighbors and friends found such distraction purposeful, and luckier still that they imputed strengths to this frail and all-too-human older man.

It had been a fierce fight—a battle to the death, to overcome all that despair in his youth—but this new, later phase seemed to be without violence because it was about choices: invisible decisions that ultimately secured him a place in a society.

There was a new man within this old man. Deep in the core of his prior self, he could recall many moments built in by evolution, deep processes that propelled him to procreate or strut about in business or even to think in creative ways about women and competition. That phase now looked hilarious. He could see all that foolishness and power in his past now, but it was fading fast.

A happy drunkenness was emerging from his deepest self. It had nothing to do with liquor, drugs, or sex. This deeper drunkenness is the source of all magical realism. He felt it almost biological, a matter of attitude and good fortune, like a burp at the right moment during a key dinner meeting. It brought magic before all. It reminded all of the sameness in us.

He remembered the old feeling when he'd look at a naked woman, where his startle response to loud noises diminished the closer he came to her flesh. This gave him a focus as intense as when in high school he approached the free-throw line: all stopped, all clapping stopped, all hooting stopped. It seemed to him now as if some chemical surge had muted something in his mind to render it less alert to danger and risk—so he could finish his job at home, to die at home well. This was the creative giddiness of self-absorption.

Most afternoons, after the morning gym routine, after a set of business calls and meetings run by reason and calm, he could stand there, as if a Hercules, readying to take a swing at time itself. On the road, days flew by. But in his home, he occupied longer, larger horizons.

At first, his dawning recognition of having been absorbed by society was an affront to his belief in self-determination: it undercut his sense of personal accomplishment, which had always been athletic, linear, effort-based. But as his top-heavy sense of competition faded, much of his good fortune now seemed to have depended on the generosity of strangers.

Yet that was part of what was so splendid about his afterlife: all the others, working for and with him, made the web shimmer. There was something deeper than chemistry going on now, something wiser than the biology of self, agitating the spider to further work on his behalf. He had achieved the ultimate revenge on life itself: he had found a way to outlive his father, and build a reputation before death in this pursuit of making capitalism itself more social, more responsive.

His sense of having been taken in, appreciated by a widening society, led him to conclude that a well-spent life required no less, and yet something more: wonder when facing the web, and a feeling of profound thankfulness for having taken a stand.

He had become a person of deep character, and certain qualities, and transcendent aspirations. He had nothing to hide as he aged, and he had a fair amount of hang time in his own personal philosophy to share still.

All his outrage, all his clubbing around for hits and impact, had dissipated into a circle of magic known as the neighborhood, a community that kept spinning him like a spider on a web. At home he did as he wished, drunk with possibilities.

THE PUSH OF HUMANITY
AT HIS DOOR

IN HIS WORK MEMOIR, *EVERYBODY MATTERS,* he used the magical techniques he had learned from his mother and grandmother to make good during times of turmoil and stress. Friends, family, firms, the clients of those firms, and *their* friends and *their* families and *their* firms sustained the web. And, as his friend Jay had suggested, "Whatever has been done can be done better"—so the web kept growing, kept shimmering, as humanity pushed at his place more and more.

He believed that great homes, like those near Ben Franklin's place in old Philadelphia, are based on this unstated trust that things can improve after a life of effort. He recalled having felt this when he visited Samuel Johnson's home in old London. He felt it again in West Hills, where Walt Whitman began his lusty ascent— these homes he described to Varlissima one long night, when they could not sleep easily.

The room was too dark, and the night too long. She tolerated the repeats in his descriptions of these Whitman and Johnson homes, for she knew they served as sedatives.

They looked at each other. The house seemed so big and empty. They took a few aspirins for their aches and pains, or sipped a bit of gin, and then, out of habit, they looked for their long-gone Colette. Then, finally, they fell asleep in the random pain of old age, his right hand resting atop her red and greying hair, hip to hip, legs scooped within each other's legs. Everyone matters; the memories were long and becoming heavier.

COLETTE AT NIGHT, AGAIN

ALTHOUGH HE WAS NOW SEVENTY-TWO, he was at times so world-weary, in the purely physical sense, that he depended on his daughter to chauffeur him around on most of the nights she was in town. This was good for her, but better for him—and best for the other drivers out there. Saratoga knew to beware his wide turns, and his absent-minded driving patterns. He was not so much dangerous as unpredictable, Colette reported.

When he would take a miserable turn, he was often thinking of a great passage from Shakespeare. A history of failure to stop properly filled his driving record. He saw a secret correlation between his speeding violations and the number of times per year he now received a note about being anthologized: it was an inverse ratio. This thought made him smile.

Varlissima had grown tired of his self-absorption and seldom ventured out with him to greet these new publics. He had traveled widely on book tours, on consulting gigs, and Varlissima rarely joined him—saving travel with him for vacations. After college, Colette would join him on the more exotic tours when she could, sometimes with her husband, and later with her kids. He would always travel with a laminated rolled-up version of the picture from her high school graduation party, as if in holding time still, he was safer somehow.

Occasionally, Darlene, who was more than two decades younger than he, would drive him around to these work obligations, dressed mostly in humble black skirts, with her stunning black hair pulled back in a ponytail. Folks came to recognize her—

she often made them smile. In recognizing her, they recognized him, who now walked slower than before, and with more of the invisibility of posture and pace that come with advanced age.

Now, at night, he was more content than seemed possible from his prior years of travel. All it took was a book and a set of memories to fall into a deeper sleep. The art of giving talks, he found, was like the art of newspaper writing. You stroked all the platitudes from your best passages, with a touch of humor, until they started to purr. He remained popular in his public outreach well into his seventies.

SACRED MEMORY

IF HE THOUGHT HARD ENOUGH about his international trips, he could sense—and then worship—the wind behind the many close calls he had experienced. It was simply marvelous to have survived so long on the road, an idler in more than a third of the world's mega-cities. This provided three new thoughts. First, his memory itself was becoming sacred, in the most appreciative way. Second, he felt, at times, in God's corner—that is, he felt advantaged by fate. Finally, he was becoming the type of lucky fool that would giggle at his own funeral—for if death came by, he had already gotten away with so much that he would not feel cheated, like his father.

When he saw Colette, Varlissima, and Darlene in the same day he felt "this is the only heaven I'll ever be invited to."

At seventy-six, it was no longer worthwhile to even count the number of places he had visited. There simply were too many to matter, or to fully recall. Since his late fifties, he did choose to go on tours of Australia, Turkey, and Ireland simply because he had never been there before. Yet now, he returned to many cities simply because he had let forty years slip by since he had last visited.

He had last walked the miracle mile that descended from Edinburgh Castle, with its crystal palace and historic prison dungeons when he was a student of Shakespeare. But now, at seventy-six, he returned to give a series of lectures on life and the business of life, and to dine with the leaders of the region. He was the same man, with the same sensibility, but now the stage had grown tremendously, and mysteriously. These returns beckoned a misty feeling in him, of high emotion, where youthful facts of sensual recollection were blended now with new sacred memories.

These recollections connected to places made him more human—so human an animal. Many recall, in later life, that when Pandora's box of travel is unhinged and then opened, the world slips out in a fashion both endless and vastly open. This now caused elation and exhaustion in the old man. There is seldom anything like a diet on the road; a whiskey diet is perhaps the closest he ever achieved consistently while traveling. Yet the great myths of old informed him about the risks he had survived, without the risk of too much whiskey. These myths of Pandora and the Midas touch helped him streamline to essence his travels. He came to accept the risks inherent in the tales of Pandora without allowing his innocence to be compromised by them. Things pop out in travel that you must reconcile, or cease to be human.

Memory was sacred in a shared universal way now, but it was also his own, vastly personal.

What remained of those memories was sacred, easily discernible if associated with images of the people along the way— the taxi driver who'd warned him off a bad neighborhood; the good friend he'd never seen again who had told him which dives to avoid and which places could be enjoyed safely; the foreign police who had helped him even without speaking his language or understanding the nature of his need. Diplomacy while traveling can be tricky, like doing fast field work with a chainsaw. But somehow, he always survived.

After the 9-11 terrorist attacks, he was met near Istanbul by men with machine guns—hating him visibly, but waving him on because he looked like a powerful American businessman. The same thing happened to him while traveling between the Turkish and Greek borders. To have survived Istanbul, Tokyo, Belfast, Melbourne, Manhattan, Paris, Rome, Canton, Sydney, Athens, Houston, Calgary, and the guns of Detroit so many times was to feel the hand of God swing past.

Each city had a marvelously different feel, an inherent personality; some were warm and exciting, others rude, troubling, and suffocating—like those Thanksgiving relatives you know too well, who cannot travel out of their ruts of idle superiority and judgment. Yet all of these great cities shared some common traits in his memory.

No matter how dismal, or dirty, or congested, the cities were growing on earth: people were surviving in great hordes, and this alone made him feel embarrassed when he arrived depressed. So he'd shed that skin like a snake, when he saw how poor and how miserable many remained. This helped him escape the worst of his American feelings. "How dare I weigh myself down when they have so much less?" he thought again and again, until he felt free of a weight around his neck.

This was a strange and effective kind of medicine. He was actually one of the lucky ones, one of those articulate few who can surround themselves with risk and find the rewards in it. People—not just his friends—now called him an optimist.

THE DRAGON ARUM

By HIS MID-SEVENTIES, he realized that anything of worth in the twenty-first century had already been destroyed by the Internet. While speed had become the order of the day, he knew that many things, like the magnificent black lily—that dragon arum—require time to bloom. Most days, there was impatience surrounding everything, from the details of a date to the reactions to a great movie.

Yet eighty percent of the century remained. Instead of the tragedy of *Romeo and Juliet* there was the wonder of *Avatar*, where flying beasts and creatures with extended legs embodied early love and longing, vying against a machine too big to turn off. Gladiatorial combat had morphed into the beautiful and improbable archery of Katniss Everdeen in *The Hunger Games*.

Technology had evolved so rapidly that everyone could play fast and loose with time: youth could see lurid shows meant for adults, and adults could settle into the fantasy of endless youth. For many, it was becoming harder and harder to turn away from the immediacy of the screen and recall actual literary experience—except for the back-to-the-earth folks who still had a backyard to roam in.

Only books could still create the sense of forgiveness and hope.

The dragon arum was a mighty strange late bloomer in his back garden—its long, oily black pistil was surrounded by a lush, deep red, almost powdery petal that caressed the pistil with close care, despite rain or storm or torture by the gardener. Privately, he had tested his dragon arums many times, trying to separate the spears from their case, but it was useless. If you broke one you broke them both. By now he felt the same way about himself and Varlissima.

It fascinated him how people made their couple-hood into something dramatic. This much was true: he and Varlissima had been late bloomers. But many couples that survive *are* late bloomers. There is so much red and black in lovers, so much magic in the fit of the pistil and the surrounding petals, that survival seems as much a matter of luck and attitude as anything.

So he paid little heed to those who assigned so much wattage to his coupling with Varlissima. He knew that Colette was the magical glue that had kept them together: she was the gift that had taken fortune's might and caressed it into a greater calm than harm. She was the girl made woman, as he was the man made old man. He began to wonder what life might have been like if he had not fathered Colette.

He came to like new neighbors and new books, and it was almost as good to meet them as to remember them. Otherwise, the weight of his mother's absence proved too much. The expected downs of old age lessened whenever he was with people—and at Old Stone Church, this turned out to be often. His yard remained large and inviting. A good book is a great leveler, and a great book a good way to silence the neighbors.

Sure, he had always pushed himself onto half of humanity, but this was how he had earned attention—how he had decided not to die too early, like his father. He would not give up that persistence, that conversational curiosity.

He was beginning to drop his defenses, to let in some wondrous, Márquez-like pirates at the gate. Until now, he had been jealous and controlling when it came to his reputation. But he really had nothing left to defend, except fun itself. His addiction to adding to the good yielded some excesses. His offices were filled with idiosyncratic icons, gifts from visitors from around the world. He groped and clutched these icons, cluttering his life with them as Freud had, in his artifact-cramped office on Vienna's Ringstrasse.

At night, he felt Varlissima, Colette, and Darlene near. Somehow aging allowed this without scandal.

He had his village. He had his jungle. He had in summer robust gardens—full of blue mouse ears that did not talk back, clusters of simple pure hearts, and abiqua drinking gourds, whose intense blue edges and emerald-green centers made him smile, both because he found their combination of colors so unexpected, and because their absorption of rain was so clever and so certain. Even with his diminishing eyesight, he still loved the petunias of his past, and still wanted his spring to bloom at Old Stone Church.

Ironically, almost magically, his surroundings at the end resembled surroundings at his start, except for all the wealth. He was with women. He was with nature. He was a man open and outside. It was all very much like living near the Long Island Railroad tracks, surrounded by women.

He was getting ready for the final resolution and choice.

MR. PLUMER, HIS TEACHER

AS HE EDGED CLOSER TO THE END OF HIS LIFE, he began to think more about the teachers who had given him his first legs, his initial standing. Without them, he might have proved a solid lawyer or a good surgeon or a rural banker. But instead he became, because of them, himself.

"Mr. Plumer was not a plumber!" He woke up one morning, saying this out loud to a startled Varlissima. This is what the class had called him—"a plumber"—when they were being mean and hurtful.

Charles Plumer was ahead of his time, and special, and rather strange for the average high school teacher. Outrage was often the start of what mattered to him. But those who got the method to Plumer's manner felt the pressure and the spray within their growing minds.

He taught Latin and great books. But it didn't really matter what Mr. Plumer taught. All truly great teachers teach love of life. The students swam with him in an atmosphere of dense, playful words—plenty of words, and for free.

Over time, Plumer's statements about writing created a set of higher facts. He claimed that at its best, writing was like building a house. Each great paragraph he fluted had a floor, a stairwell, some walls, and a set of bright, well-framed windows to the world.

One day, out of the blue, Plumer said, "It takes two floors to make a story." Having grown up in a small, two-floored home near the railroad tracks, he knew exactly what his teacher meant. The best stories have several floors and are rarely linear, despite what so many teachers required. The best stories draw the reader into the future by creating a presence that allows a sense of the past. The best stories create a mansion of meanings.

He could run up Plumer's arguments all day long, smelling for hints like a dog on a stairwell, and then jump back down them swiftly, without hurting himself.

This was how he learned that teaching was about extending one's reach. Plumer's stories always led to another story, and then another. This was how Plumer had taught early experimentation with vast mansions of meaning.

In the end, he owed his sense of architectonics in writing to Charles Plumer. He learned that he could build a structure that was like memory itself, and as magical as life itself—if he pushed the Pause and Fast Forward buttons enough. Charles Plumer taught him what mattered: the sound of the words, and the ability to outrage. Plumer saw eye to eye with the greats, like Twain and Melville, in both anger and in hope.

He related to Plumer as if he had been his lost father. When he was fifteen years old, Plumer had told him out of the blue that he would be a good father someday. Now that he was much older he realized what an insightful risk that proved.

Charles Plumer did not help him remember formulas or see the stars more clearly or even appreciate Shakespeare. Plumer helped him develop a spirit of observation, a sense of belonging anywhere—that is, wherever he felt at play.

OLD AGE
AT THE LOTOS CLUB

WERE IT NOT FOR THE LOTOS CLUB, and its distinct company of friends, old age might have proven dreary at times. But whenever he felt he needed to jazz up his calm at Old Stone Church, he'd hop on a train to Manhattan, and make his way to 5 East 66th Street. It was from there a quick walk to Central Park, with its buzz of hills achievable at any age. And visiting the Frick Collection always worked to give him a tick up, as did visiting the shows at the Armory. "There was a very long afternoon to life if you could visit such a club," he thought.

Thanks to Charles Plumer's training, he had been inducted as a member of Mark Twain's Lotos Club in Midtown Manhattan in his fifties, right after *Doing More With Less* became listed as a *New York Times* bestseller.

From factory boy to member of this elite literary club, he never changed. It was his perception of others that matured. While he had a bad habit of dropping names to make his public talks dramatic and people based, rather than concept based, he now had the chance to watch people whose life achievements made his efforts sensible. He had always felt exactly like a stranger in the paradise of academia, but at this club he felt he had a home away from home.

He was always the same guy from Long Island, always the kid who'd grown up near the railroad tracks, but he needed to work out the boastfulness that business had built and hardwired into him. In business, you get more chances by being bold; but in the life of the mind, in the day to day at the club, it might prove the reverse. It was the perception of others that had ripened so much in him, adding a quiet humility when he sat in the internal garden of the Frick, eyeing real wealth. This was humility at its best.

Now he was among many accomplished people at the club, and from time to time they helped him ready for old age. This was the real value in its membership to him, not the fine welcomes, fresh meals, and outstanding rooms. Now the richness was mostly in a conversation with a few accomplished people, who didn't need to ask for anything, but instead lived lives of a more quiet resolution, with tea in the afternoon. He now had many fine talks at noon, where he listened to Robert Caro recall state dinners and tell tales of President Johnson, and heard Gay Talese and Tom Wolfe reinvent the New Journalism, as both memory and achievement.

The process of being proposed, elected, and then honored lasted over a year, and involved secretly solicited reviews of both character and ambition. Since he never felt that he'd be elected, that year passed in pleasant travel for work and discovery. But becoming a member changed everything for him, as it worked its magic and he went from ceaselessly wanting to mostly enjoying watching the members talk.

The first time he entered this place of beautiful stillness and history he came upon the bust of Mark Twain, which stared across the first lounge at a painting of the same author. He was sure this placement of the two Twains was very deliberate.

"How appropriate," he could hear Charles Plumer saying. Plumer did not admire the accomplished as much as appreciate them, in all their human frailty. "Is it not true that accomplished writers are always looking at themselves?" Plumer whispered in his ear.

He experienced one of those near-death dreams that prepared him for a deeper and more wondrous old age. . . . What he remembered best about Charles Plumer was a final class in Latin. It proved his first rite of passage into a writer's life. The class had spent most of the spring translating the poetry of Catullus, Homer, and Ovid, and Cicero's Orations. That day, Plumer had taken out some replicated maps showing a Roman hunting camp from 300 AD.

Even in his eighties, he could picture the scene vividly. He was sitting behind Mary Beth, whose left shoulder carried a most lovely "you-need-to-stroke-this" beauty mark. The camp caught his eye over Mary Beth's contoured and tanned teenage shoulder.

Mimicking the posture and tone of a Roman instructor, Plumer held up a photo of a decorative tile from the hunting camp and said, "Now, ever-earnest Dr. Piasecki, please translate this image before us, and render it from Latin into English for the awaiting class." The request clinched his future as a writer, right then and there.

"The woman's rotund butt was naked," he said in his head. He knew the translation was accurate, but he also felt that he was in the middle of a Fellini film, watching as many others watched him. He loved this feeling, the words in his head.

He could see the translation in his head, but could he say it out loud? Finally, he said loudly, "The woman's rotund butt is naked." The class roared. He was a star.

NORAH JONES,
FAITH, AND THE FABULOUS

THERE WAS NOW SOMETHING SACRED IN THREES. Father-Son-Holy Ghost type stuff. The flight-of-an-eagle, stare-of-a-hawk, speed-of-a-falcon type stuff. Varlissima-Colette-Darlene type stuff. Firms-families-friends type stuff. Now-then-near future type stuff. Seeing things in threes enhanced his fun.

He had spent five decades learning the art of comparison, of two things in parallel, love of daughter with love of wife. But now he was seeing it all in a more Biblical trinity.

Music helped this triple lens descend, like grace and force and fascination. The voice of Norah Jones had helped bring it to a peak. He always had an interest in something that was at the pinnacle of many things he liked, and when it came to voice, Norah's sat at the top for him, so haunting, so exact, so smooth, so certain, so pronounced.

The more he listened the more he could hear the distinct swooping in Norah's voice. He could, at last, hear a distinction between small Asian vultures, fish eagles, and African buzzards without binoculars. As if her voice was visibly distinct, he paused each time he heard her. Her voice was that good. There was a longevity in the flight of some birds of prey; there was a certainty in the heights and slaughter of Norah Jones' profound songs.

In threes, he got closer to the infinite found deep inside his soul. Ironically, the numbers 88 did the same for him, giving him an instant dipstick to the infinite. To be 8 is to offer him a favorite number, but to have him think of 88 is to glimpse the eternal, and with 888, he began a pattern he could contemplate with a sense of the religious becoming spiritual. When Colette was a mere child, they would joke about who first chose the number 8 as their favorite number.

"Things come in threes when magical," he intoned. Large Australian hawks he and Colette had seen together during a 2012 book tour of Sydney's Blue Mountains, were better when matched with memories of New Guinea soaring hawks, and best if matched in the mind with American Eagles. Things were good in themselves, couplings had perspective, but threes gained a kind of magnificence.

The magic was in the distinctions and the parallels of threes. Things that come in threes make logic limited, and computers dumb. Self-interest is impossible in the realm of threes—and proves unnecessary, even though it had once constituted much of what he was about, in the realm of business.

Now he had the time for amazement. Many of the birds of prey, notably the larger eagles of America, some North American sparrowhawks and goshawks, harriers and falcons, had been cited extensively by Varlissima and him. (Being by nature sportive in the atmosphere of beauty, he had always jokingly referred to goshawks as "gosh-hawks," extending the second "H" like Norah does deliciously in some of her best short songs. Why? Hell, to extend the sounds on extended wings.)

When he told his doctors about seeing things in threes, one suggested they were floaters in his eyes. He never went again to that legendary doctor, feeling him resigned for retirement.

He wondered: Could he remember even half of the people who stood before him, those in his office, smiling near? At this point, it did not seem to matter as much as keeping three delightful visitors in mind at once, comparing their natures in a bright triangle, and then spinning the triangle in his idle brain.

In the main trends of evolution. a kite becomes either a snake eagle or a harrier hawk before ghosting its prior self into a goshawk. It was a long time in evolution before we got the harpy eagles and now the booted eagles he and Varlissima had come to love and watch. These were not so much plays on words as plays on time, for once you know enough about memory, you can manipulate the pace and sequence to get the three things you delightfully prefer.

It is all in your mind, after all, something Marcus had taught him to control.

Where exactly do these songs of Norah Jones get etched into our minds anyway, that he could hum them after so many years? And *when* exactly do these memories of people long gone, like his mother, decide to matter? *Where's the threshold*, and *who* designs the filters? Neuroscience was beginning to uncover some answers. He began reading intensively in that budding field.

He flew with these thoughts every time he heard the songs of Norah Jones. This elongation of his memory was there, also, whenever he re-watched a movie by Fellini, or read a passage by his lifelong friend Jay Parini. Someday, yes he'd get to it; he'd write an essay comparing "The Fancy of Fellini and a Friendship With Parini." Meanwhile, he'd keep reading neuroscience, and reading about hawks and eagles and other birds of prey.

He concluded that creative memory is the glue that fixes faith with the fabulous, which joins friends and family in the higher forms of memory. This formed a circle of missing persons that had become somehow sacred. Strangely, his contemplation of this sacredness often involved threes.

This allowed a new appreciation of Norah Jones—her voice so heavy yet so light—a new appreciation of faith itself, and a deeper appreciation of the fabulous.

SUCCESS AT HOME

FOR AT LEAST TWO DECADES, he had been preparing to die at sea. That would fit the image of the drunken Hercules, and set sail to the notion that he was merely a fortunate homebody who had made good. During several trips overseas, he had eyed a piece of land near the coast of Sicily, and near the same hill that Virgil had climbed every summer to escape the disease of the coastal swamps.

Varlissima had eyed the same town—Erice, just up the hill from Trapani, where all the homes had both bad plumbing and out-of-this-world views. These homes were made from the same magical, absolutely beautiful, locally quarried Sicilian stone. "Strong and steady," they thought, each time they visited these stone homes. Everyone was in rare agreement: Colette saw that the town was special. They all felt "the surprise" there.

So at eighty-three, limping on the cobblestones that led up to this small plaza with a spectacular view, he was allowed to buy—with Varlissima's approval—their second stone home. At his advanced age, the grand sameness of all these homes would lead him, several times, to visit the wrong home, where he would end up in delightful unintended conversations, usually in English.

He and Varlissima settled near the top of the hill from which Virgil had watched the wars of Peloponnese. On some nights, as they sat together, they could watch ships nearing the coast, much as Virgil did in his recollections of the North African and Greek positioning in ancient wars.

"Adventure is gratuitous unless brought home for sharing." He came to thank Herman Melville for having taught him that. As he wandered to exotic places, he always brought them back to Old Stone Church Road. Thoughts of Erice were more like memories of a vacation than experiences of a second home. There was no second home, in fact, except on the balance sheets.

He had first gotten the idea of appropriating the world when he visited Sigmund Freud's Vienna home: it was filled with the totems that the doctor would then shred to pieces, stuffing them back into his most mesmerizing theories and books.

Success at home, he now saw, was about bringing the world within his own boundary conditions. And intelligence was about feeling good about that—feeling accomplished by being scaled back into satisfaction.

He did not, in the end, need the full world; all he really needed was a good place from which to compose his world. The persistence to get past home while at home was the ultimate key.

At eighty-eight, he imagined himself placing the two numbers for infinity next to each other. The number eighty-eight made sense. He was ready to die that year, but he did not. It took great persistence, this aging process, where urine and digestion and standing straight become big things. All of this proved tolerable for someone who stayed true to his home.

He and Varlissima kept the Bentley estate for their child, for her children, and for her children's children, just as the Bentleys had done for seven generations before them. This proved rare in the new America, but it was something he had wanted from the first time he heard Uncle Ziggy talk about the old country

By good fortune, he returned many times to his home on Old Stone Church Road. The lawn looked better than ever before. Was it the new forms of targeted fertilizer? Or was it simply his failing eyesight?

At a dinner party for his eighty-ninth birthday, the lovely Varlissima slipped a strange quote from D.H. Lawrence into the proceedings, reading it aloud with a knowing quiver in her eyebrows:

> *I can never decide whether my dreams are the result of my thoughts, or the thoughts are the result of my dreams. It is very queer. But dreams make conclusions for me. They decide things finally. I dream a decision. Sleep seems to hammer out for me the logical conclusions of my vague days, and offer me them as dreams.*

Having survived him for so many decades, Varlissima was saying, in her wonderful indirect way, that she had come to see that most of his life he was not decisive as much as a dreamer—and that, perhaps, is what she had loved in him.

THE LAST OBSESSION

THE LAST OBSESSION INVOLVES THE FACE OF DEATH, time's most constant mistress and its final formidable friend. He could not out-talk her, he could not out-walk her. He must lie next to her, and watch his remaining breaths.

Decades of action repress the fear of death; this was why, he believed, some of his peers remained addicted to business long after having gained sufficient wealth. But she resurfaces, mocking us with her silk see-through pantaloons. Even those born with grace and force cannot outlast her fascination.

He already knew that many are hurt—and had found ways to say, with Emily Dickinson, "But, what of that?" He already knew that life is short. But again, what of that?

Despite all this, he witnessed the pursuit of a new equation: investments in genetic means of extending life, the restoration of broken limbs, the search for new ways to get even, to shimmy off her pantaloons and say, "Ha, I told you I could outwit you." But, near the end, he knew that none of this could be sustained, and that death was impossible to master.

Some call the fascination with death the source of all creative effort. Others size her up as if a fine Elizabethan clock, that mocks us as it ticks away.

Like Jung, he found his wealth in an understanding of death's many costumes. His final obsession told him that the Book of Job is open to its most haunting chapters beneath most business dealings, beside most intimate relationships, and in every honest memoir. Death is the dance that none can outlast.

Yet the beach where he was born suggested that he might live on in his works, in the dreams of his daughter, in his hopes for a faultless company succession.

So much of his wealth had seemed contingent, once, on his own enterprising will, and the grace of good fortune. So much of him seemed dispersed in memories now. In the end, no savvy investment advisor or brilliant estate attorney had any lasting answer. They were as ineffective, despite their big fees, as Job's friends.

Half the trouble with this obsession was caused by the will—the force that had driven him into his fantasy of near futures in the first place. However fascinated by will or intrigued by endless, receding horizons, all must pay the fee to cross over to another shore. Varlissima was the one he had elected to be by his side.

He knew all this at first: before college, before competition, before success. But he waited for her to confirm it in him. There had been so much pleasure in pretending to forget this last obsession.

This last obsession brought him back, in the end, to Old Stone Church. He was at home in this place; he knew its winds and its history, and that it was his part of the world. Varlissima remained his wonder woman at Old Stone Church because she had liberated this last obsession in him from the start, even during his first days with her at Cornell, knowing his defiant youth to be his answer to the nearing face of death. He had come to believe that she had stuck with him for all those decades because he was willing to forge ahead, and embrace each day with her.

He could see the face of death more clearly now, without distraction. She came constantly nearer each day, to shave him even, and to clip his ever-harder toenails. He could feel her satisfy him, eating him to the core with her stare of disapproval or her smile. Either brought him close to the same end. And while he hated this obsession, he knew that its splendidly focused, incredible rightness would win.

GOOD READING
BECOMES HIS MISTRESS

THE SIMPLE ACKNOWLEDGEMENT OF AGING can be as swift as it is severe. It was impossible to repel: age continued to attack, like Mongol invaders whose round eyes never seemed to sleep.

After a while, all the insults of aging looked the same: insistent. He was no sultan after all, neither in business nor in life, despite the land holdings and his vast-imagined legacy. He was simply another man, and an old one at that. Consciously and willingly, he entered the final seasons.

He knew that life would carry on in his absence. Little on his property would be affected by his death. The money tree would likely remain standing, or most of it. The butterfly garden would continue to bloom in the spring, amid the sound of the peepers and the katydid's soulful song.

Throughout his decades at Old Stone Church, the five winds of change had lifted the descending leaves—sometimes for as long as ten minutes—into the chilled air of his back gardens; but eventually they would fall, only to rise again before hitting the ground, along with their muted and identical sisters. There was no real, lasting human lesson in watching the leaves fall. There was no real value in counting the blades of grass each spring. The home and the church were his answer.

Varlissima had warned him not to get too attached to this home. She said they needed to be prepared to sell it at any time; for if it became too big to maintain, she would kill him before the house killed her!

He now remembered Varlissima's prediction, as they signed their mortgage a few months before Colette's birth. She said the home would witness the three inevitable stages of every couple's sex life: first there is house sex, when they are newly infatuated with the place and have sex all over the house. Then there is bedroom sex, when they allow the routine only in the bedroom to protect the children. The final stage, she predicated, is hall sex—when they've been married so long they just pass each other in the hallway and shout, "Fuck you!"

He looked for his antecedents under the soles of his boots, and never found them except when at home. Walt was not his father after all, but a smart hint at what a father could be. Wordsworth's child of man was only intimation, another form of transfiguration. It all became a matter of degrees, of vital signs and small differences, amid a vast universe of similarities in what was claimed to be humanity.

There was now so much more than mere humanity available in his backyard.

THE WIND
IN HIS BACKYARD

THERE WERE FIVE CORNERS TO HIS PROPERTY. The Old Stone Church, his home itself, the company offices, and the old barn were peaked by a fifth corner where the prior owner's wife had constructed a small building to sing her operas. These five corners defined the property from which he did his earning, growing, and sharing.

These five corners produced the winds of change that had always stood strong behind him—waving him on, tempting a boy from West Islip to ask the bigger questions—while the Old Stone Church stood solid, defying his tiny ambition with its stone certainty. The uneven rock face reminded him, daily, that it, not him, was proud testimony to the passing of even the strongest winds. It had stood there, quietly, since 1824.

There was something deep and astonishing about wind—something that kept him going, pushing him from behind, something that did not destroy his hope. It said: *"Fervor is more important than fame, zeal more worthy than worth."* He had never read this in a book, yet he felt this mantra deep as part of his heart, pumping his blood.

Wind was worldly, event-based, and more mysterious than formal thought. Where once only women dwelled, the wind now formed a source of his inspiration. Whenever sick, he simply found a way outside and sat with the wind, cup of tea in hand, cigar unlit, and soon felt better.

He saw that his proportionate, ego-based self—the self by which he had been measuring his accomplishments and bankbook—had operated under a recurrent, insistent, functional deception, an illusion of certainty, despite the fact that some things are beyond proportion, like wind.

"What if the things that matter most, in the end, are beyond measure? Is that the best way to define God?" he asked.

Boldly overweight and overworked, he stood as if against a final wall that held him up. He leaned into his next thinking—as one leans into the wind when it blows bitter cold.

But this time the wind was warm, and the lean comfortable. He said, "The computational self, the self that measured what mattered in the everyday, that calculated and assigned value to things, had been a strong force in youth"—but as he aged into this new stance, he began to round things off and to wonder where wind comes from, and why it is usually there, but invisible, subtle, and intractable. There are even winds, he felt now, that only follow rivers.

He loved all this whirling around the Old Stone Church: the simple way the wind spoke to him in the fall and winter—shaking his trees, and at times threatening to bring down the old twisted limbs and trunk of the money tree, but never really bothering to do it.

Life was now all about his backyard; it was all about the wind, about the wind's temporary resistance to the deeper meanings that meant we were alive.

FURTHER READING
ABOUT THE WORLD

HE WAS TRAVELING A GREAT DEAL LESS NOW, so his retreat into memory mounted. . . .

He remembered the scene in Vienna vividly—the slow inquiring pace with which she approached. She was nameless; he was in his twenties. He could remember every curve of her shape, the length of her shaven thighs, the bones of her hips that protruded beyond her flat belly, the beauty mark on her neck—such an odd place—that spoke his language. But all he could recall of her clothes was that she was not dressed in the ugly reds of America. She had perfect lips, perfect hips, and a neck worth holding.

She was able to press her lips against the glass of his Viennese friend's car, and not speak his language, yet still seduce. How was all this possible? How could he have lived through all that past, that long sensual middle, and still be around to think about it all again?

When he held her neck now in memory, he knew that true leaders were self-appointed. Gandhi in India was not the same man as Gandhi in his memoirs or at home. Nelson Mandela in South Africa was not the same man in his memoirs or at the United Nations. Distortion is inevitable as we move through time—this self-invention, this revision, this delightfully windy sense of self and self-worth. If you repress this wind at the center of fervor, you can never be free, never create something the world did not know how to ask for.

The sun spoke to him through all this mist. She whispered something in his ear. She whipped her chin, with a foreign smile, and began down the road toward the Ringstrasse, never to be with him again until just now.

She must have originally been from a deeper east—perhaps Russian or a mix of Russian and Asian. Her name sounded to him, that day in Vienna, like Maya. His friend let her in and left the car; the rest was memory. All his readings in history could not dispel her, could not alarm her, could not warm her; and all his learning did not need to erase her.

Another of his memories would rise from the bed and brush her teeth afterwards, another had bad feet, a third wore hats that were about ten times the worth of her jeans, which she flung to the floor without request or longing.

Memories were becoming great books—immensely pleasurable, but now also far off, as if beyond the importance of the actual people who first wrote them. A shelf could seem miles away these days. When he looked over the books of those he had met: Gay Talese with the tall tales of his immigrant father; Tom Wolfe with his bold and flamboyantly certain prose; Robert Caro, whose historic detail was as exact and recurrent as the movements of a trained swimmer—they seemed decades away now. He would get up from his reading to reach for another, knees cracking.

Good reading became his best mistress.

KARL MARX
AND HIS NURSE

WITH AGE, HE REALIZED THE THEORIES that had fascinated him in youth could prove a joke. Take his imaginary neighbor Karl Marx, for example. Karl was a great reader—from the time he was first spotted in the Reading Room of the British Museum, until he arrived at the Old Stone Church in a wheelchair. The creak of the chair was audible even from across the pond in winter, and the sound of his breathing machines proved pronounced, a constant background. His powers had waned as he lost mobility, and the entire world followed the pattern of his decline.

Meanwhile, strangely, capitalism continued to flourish across a growing world as Marx began to fade. As Asia found some dragons, and Brazil and Turkey and the former Soviet states rose to market force, Karl's first thoughts became dimmer and dimmer. It was as if his entire worldview had had a stroke.

He was a fighter, and would give hell to his nurses and aides. Rather than preaching in five-year plans, Karl made requests by the hour, sometimes seven requests in ten minutes. He would sit in his chair, shaking a bit from the excess of medications the market gave him at low cost, barking out orders to his aides, until someone thought that perhaps someone else had complied.

For Bruce, perhaps because he had read too many books by Marx and Tolstoy in his youth, this imaginary Karl remained a terror to his dying day. And yet Karl's aging made his own aging easier to take. At least he had written some books that remained in line with where the world was going.

SELDOM SEEN IN
SARATOGA

THE PAPER-THIN KATYDIDS RETURNED faithfully each summer to the trees lining Old Stone Church Road.

Remorse was his favorite emotion because its half-life was long—longer in its screeching certainties than the katydids' eggs that hide on the bark of the twigs in his backyard. The tiny nymphs hatch each spring, and most find mates mathematically, as they mature in the heat and moisture that gathers near Saratoga during the dog days of late summer.

The katydids danced outside his living room windows, making loud, screeching, protest sounds. Seldom seen in Saratoga, they were populous at his homestead.

True to their name, these *Pterophylla camellifolia* were normally camouflaged in the many large oaks near Old Stone Church. If he listened hard at night, he could discern their song, even over the relentless peepers in the pond next door.

Like most relatives of grasshoppers and crickets, the true katydids are best known for the call of the males, bolder than Shakespeare's Hotspur. Loud, rasping notes—worse than teenagers in heat—the bugs would appear in late June, right after his Corporate Affiliates had left town. He was able to be quiet again, then, and listen to the sound coming from the broad-leafed trees. The ground-floor windows were wide open—just as they must have been open in the early years of the house—and some of the katydids would cling to the meshed windows.

By the height of track season in Saratoga, their chorus would become a deafening crescendo that would last throughout the night; but by early fall, only a few males would continue to call. In the cold night air, they seem to call with a delayed and dignified dejection.

The ones still calling were those that had failed to find mates. They would cling to his study windows as he turned off the light. Those rare males were the ones he was most attracted to. Sensing a loss that is not yet there was a rich way to earn winter's alertness, the katydids said to him each summer.

The katydid dies, its bright green wings crossed with the heavy veins of time. You can find the casing near the trees after spring. Meanwhile, the long antenna of remorse lives on.

TITILLATING
THE AMYGDALA

ONE GIRL CURLED UP ON HIS LAP most effectively in windowsills, sucking them both into sleep. In those early days, he didn't really need a comfortable bed. Now he needed his memories to fall back to sleep.

Another girl—the only accurate term for a woman who acted younger than her college years—longed explicitly for his athletic embrace, seeking titillation by resisting. She would roll over at last, and it was clear she had aroused herself by believing in him. He recalled even after sixty years the exact size of her green eyes. There was mock fear in her, like in Japanese Kabuki. Later she would marry one of his friends.

He had seen that pattern before, long before, in Hurricane Sandy. That girl followed him through life. He had watched her, with her four husbands, conceive a rich set of lovely, curly-haired children. As in a Márquez narrative, each generation for Sandy became even more beautiful, in a classic Russian sense. Memories of Sandy and Frida still titillated his amygdala, which sent off signals creating more memories, and more satisfaction, in his vast past.

He felt the memory of these women made him better somehow, that their valor had claim to how he did not waste his life. They enabled him to write books for smart people, for modern people who knew that something was wrong about the times, yet that there was also something very right about the modern sense of the multivalence in relationships, and the diversity of coupling in families. What was sweetest about the memories of these missing persons was that they were vivid.

His hottest girlfriend once convinced him, as they hitched across the Mountain States, to carry her naked on his back at night, in a long march through some aspen woods. The next morning, as they ascended a steep grade in the bright, light-green of the quaking aspen, they gasped to see that the way back entailed a 300-foot drop, straight onto the bed of a rushing river.

It was titillating to remember such close calls. Hollywood prefers happy endings because until death, all memories are fundamentally of survival. At ninety-six, the memory of these encounters proved priceless. The vibrant, bubble gum-pink clusters of roses near his back door still bloomed. They were called Knock Outs; just dig a hole and the little stars would keep blooming nonstop from early spring through fall—disease resistant, and forever young.

THE BEACH WHERE
HE WAS BORN

THE BEACH WHERE HE WAS BORN and the beach where he became a man were one and the same: the Robert Moses Beach Three on Long Island.

However old he became, his memories of those beach days were always golden, always solid. It was here that he never felt alone, as the endlessly shifting sands were his own. It was here that his fears disappeared during long walks along the coast, as if personal harms were fiction and the story line of his life was mostly and essentially good.

There could be a thousand others near his side, but he could still feel content at his beach. It was here that he brought Varlissima at her charming best, his daughter Colette at her finest, his mother, and his muses. The beach never disappointed them— seldom left them with a dark impression, despite brutal storms and fierce ocean winds.

The salt on his face was saving. Here he met the wind, caressed the surf, chased with stern gestures the terns and other coastal birds until they looked at him with idle suspicion, heads tilted sideways and legs readied for flight.

Urged on by the music of the beach, by its simple cadence, he shared the same breath with the beach. It was the beach where he was born, after all; the beach where he remained a man.

THE INCREDIBLE RIGHTNESS
OF RESOLVE

HE WAS NINETY-SIX, alert to the vastness beside him, which he could still glimpse when shopping for books on Manhattan's Upper East Side. He was now thankful, knowing that he could never possibly read what he had acquired.

Books were his native universe—he came to see some as his private deer dances, sending him smoke signals and warnings. He began to sign his name on page ninety-six for fun, as it was his secret page, an ancient signal that would help Colette seek out honest borrowers from book sharks after he was soon gone. Books were, in the end, his portfolio of dreams worth cultivating. He never lent a book without expecting it back. Most other things he gave away with abandon, never expecting them back.

Oscar Wilde had noted that "there is no such thing as a moral or an immoral book. Books are either well-written, or badly written." There was no hero in this library of his, only charming and life-affirming books. Twain was as right as Wilde: "A thick old fashioned heavy book is the finest thing in the world to startle a noisy cat."

With a sense of mounting irony, he also now knew that it was books—not his original family—that had developed his soul for society. . . his final resting place.

HIS SUCCESSION PLANS

COLETTE HAD KIDS, and her kids had kids. Unlike him, they all enjoyed child-bearing when they were half the age he was when he had Colette, and what a wise move that was! His Old Stone Church estate remained his domain, as the generations came by now. Call this dumb luck or resolve: it had all become enough.

He was beginning to understand why the best estate plans see three generations out, or more, and he celebrated in his soul their terms for "contingent" generations—what superbly absurd wording for extended financial love.

Something still mattered with a rightness that he wanted to capture and to explain to his descendants. But he could not—except in anecdotes and vignettes—share this valuable something. He would assemble the family, mutter a few things. They still wanted figures and promises from the old man. It was not that they were the three daughters of King Lear. They were merely seeking clarity, which he lacked. Was it simply his shortness of breath, or perhaps his stubbornness of mind, that prevented the full family explanation? Perhaps it was the silencing effects of death herself. So, often, he refused to give too much detail in each account, even to Bonnie Jones, his estate attorney. Varlissima would get red in the face out of embarrassment. He had negotiated the executors, and sometimes changed them on what seemed like a whim.

During recent years, he felt that he had captured, on rare occasions, this elusive guest, this meaning of meanings, when she would visit him at the beach or in his bed with the warm breath of a stallion. He liked this muse of death to visit more and more, her black strength of a ponytail hovering near him. To hell with practicality when she walked near. He knew it was odd and corny, like the Western songs that celebrate the stance of a woman or how she works—but death had her allure now, like in those songs. He felt this way now about the approach of death. She would stand near him until he was satisfied, and then jolt off, Whitman's gigantic beauty of a stallion all his own up close. Fantasy was physical, at times.

He decided that in coming home, he had been given the best clue to his family's destiny. This made him feel even better than his succession plans and the gifts structured across Colette's children's children's lives. He knew that his money would be felt by them, but he could not really feel them that far out, although he often tried. During his business days he had said "money is meaningless if projected too far," and now he knew the personal depth of that higher fact.

Instead of exact projections, along the shorelines of his memory, all boats sailed—as they were, as they had been, at ease, shimmering in his mind. Everyone matters, so he would share as much as made tax sense to others, not his family only. Mother, father, friends past and present, sisters, his daughter—they all shimmered now, magnificent and near.

The lighting storm of his recall was refined like an athlete's muscles, transporting him a bit faster and further than ever before, until his universe seemed as if it was passing him by. But he knew, as he walked the coastlines of his finest memories, he knew he would watch Colette's final wave of goodbye soon, as he stood unable to move against that wall of time.

She was his legacy, his final pleasant textual passage to the world.

This, at last, was what made him whole.

FINALE

HE IMAGINED HIS
READERS

HE DID NOT KNOW WHEN HE WOULD DIE. She would call him, this lovely siren, even touch his weaker arm early some mornings with a tingle, asking him to join her and her lovely set of friends.

Each friend would have a new wet curve to dash before him; a new storyline to tempt him. He had learned an important thing: that humankind has not woven the web of life, but that each of us is merely a thread within that greater web. And eventually, he would glide into this stronger, lasting realm, feeling the sticky and sincere connections of life and death itself. Getting to the ancients, becoming one of them during his mature years, was like touching the synapses within his own brain now. He could feel their warmth, their surprising closeness of tradition and change, their sharp corrections from A to Z in a memory, their constant rewiring, even while he was still alive. Memory is life's most astute accomplishment.

He could only dream about it, this thing called death, and it added vivid colors to his life, even at ninety-six, and a delirious intensity to his anticipated remaining days. His brain felt, at last, believable.

Every third thought he had now was a memory. More and more each day, the images that floated in his mind as he rested recalled the sirens calling him into sleep. The logic of lyric filled his days and nights.

They were lovely, these muses of death. They were his newest friends.

COLETTE DISCOVERS
THIS MEMOIR

THAT OCTOBER MORNING, HER BREASTS WERE WARM. This muse, however worldly she appeared, wore the rightness of his home inside her. The scent of the musty leaves of Old Stone Church's many oaks and maples were blended with the astral perfumes of this nearing but not nursing muse.

A bad heart, a bad set of eyes, ears half forgotten, and a set of twisted neck nerves—these were the things of his physical life now. Yet his spiritual life, when shared with other people, was at an all-time high. In fact, these higher facts of people and their nature were making him into a man who lived often under the total absorption of a reader lost in a great book.

His plan this day was to reread *The Tempest*. He held in his hand the Folio Society's 450th anniversary edition of the book, designed by a team of giants, to celebrate the Bard's birthday.

The choice allowed him, despite his poor eyesight, to read again about Prospero and his daughter in a relaxed manner, to reread the familiar words without eyes wandering from text to comment, in a fine paper crispness. This made the book itself have the force of a personality, not to mention the words of Shakespeare. Baskerville letterpress type remains one of the most timeless of English typefaces, he felt, and he felt the people of Folio had designed the book for his hands.

It was as if book printer Stan Lane knew Prospero, as well. And it was as if he knew, for sure, that some distinct day, after his death, that his only daughter, Colette, would reread his work while he was gone. The quality of that thought, as he held this particular book, proved poignant to him. They both—the book and the thought—gave him hope, somehow, that Colette would know his work someday.

Varlissima tried to wake him from this reading.

He held on tightly to the long, heavy book.

The marbling effect of the past and the present were like the droplets of oil that floated in the printing solution of carrageen moss that allowed, at the right temperature, this special, dream-like quality to the paper and the tale.

He'd roam his hand over these book covers during dreamy afternoon naps like he had once roamed the sensual curves of his lovers. Yes, he said to himself—he had been hand marbled by women, making each of his books unique, but all of a human pattern. He was not shaking outside now; he was shaking inside.

He was descending into a depth in tradition that showed him how superficial and wanting all his work remained—that is, superficial if compared to the tradition now in his lap. He was glad that he had left the study of Shakespeare to others. For the study of the Bard could have consumed his entire life, as it did some of his classmates. What mattered now was if Colette might at an older age reread his works. That was all that mattered this day. It was becoming an agitated dream, like the ones he had during those nights when he first dreamt of Frida.

Varlissima was now telling him that this was a special day: Colette would be visiting with her now thirty-year old daughter, Ariel.

But he had fallen into a deep, almost misty sleep, still clutching *The Tempest*.

He was trying, in this dream, to convey something urgent to his daughter, and now to Ariel beside her. His dream became verbal:

"If you have a redemptive imagination, Ariel and Colette, and if you both care to make something out of the rest of your lives, beyond money, and influence, and prestige, you may sense in these books on my shelves some roots to family longevity."

He had not felt such urgency to get through to his only daughter since she had decided on her first college. He felt, in this dream, that she understood what he meant about a redemptive imagination, and this made him feel warm, and thankful.

. . . He fell into a deeper, hotter sleep, still clinging to *The Tempest*. Colette chatted with Varlissima outside his room. They were drinking jasmine tea. They could still talk, intimately, for hours. He had sometimes been jealous of this mother-to-daughter closeness; but now he felt it all good, and sensible, and even wonderful.

The wind collected outside.

Colette had discovered his memoir the day before. With her mom and daughter near, Colette had flipped through the passages addressed to her in his books. She understood him like never before.

What a persistent bastard he had turned out to be, Varlissima had hinted during that afternoon chat—both to Colette, and surprisingly, to Ariel. He had been suffering from vertigo since 2007, but the family had never let that settle in, as he kept traveling, as he kept earning, as he kept writing for decades after that. This made him hard to live with at times. Perhaps the dream irritation was a result of this advanced vertigo.

After Colette left that night, he deeply regretted missing her and Ariel.

In the middle of that night, he thought vividly about the Japanese portrayal of longevity: three perfectly white cranes—one for family, one for action, and one for memory. Beautifully engraved icons revealed all three to be intimately related. He wished desperately that before he died he could convey to Colette, and perhaps the younger Ariel, the incredible rightness of family, since he knew he never got it right in one spot in any of his books. But now this wrongness felt right, like when finding a glorious passage in a book!

Science would change, profits would wither, friendships might go missing, love itself might prove forgotten; but this figure-eight of family, action, and memory had the promise of our future.

Finale

He was so glad he had brought up this idea of a redemptive imagination during Colette's life. He felt it shouldn't be hidden, the way that some parents hide from discussing sex or love itself.

Colette now saw the connections in his work and in his life—she was beginning to know what he had worked so hard to know. She knew as well how little we can capture in a single life, and she came to find he had tried the best he could. She would do the same.

In all this he lived on, feeling again that he had achieved a resolution that might last.

HOMES, HOPE, AND
THE HIDDEN

COSMOLOGISTS AND PHYSICISTS at Harvard and MIT claimed that only about 4 percent of the universe could be seen. What was in all the darkness, he wondered, that was hidden from everyone?

It was neither family, nor fame, nor hope. But what was it? It was odd, he thought, as he'd read about neuroscience and astral physics, that he had come to weave together a new sense of hope, and its relationship to what is hidden from life.

The scientists said that the unseen consisted of dark matter and dark energy—something yet to be discovered. This holds all that can be seen in a kind of suspension. The invisible keeps the visible in gravitational equilibrium—like memories in the aging self—preventing the whole damned thing from collapsing inward into nothingness.

At age ninety-six, this exclamation and scientific claim seemed to him as grand a theory as any, to correct and recalibrate the popular sense of self. Life was the composite of all the missing persons one has known. That was identity; that was biography. And with hope and glue, friends, like readers, extended who he was.

To define identity as concentric circles of the self—id, ego, superego, friends, family, firm, with each circle getting slightly larger and encircling all the prior forms of the self—was the most naïve thing he had ever heard. That was merely a material self, whereas the proportionate self, and the aspiring self, lived on, beyond logic, in a new logic of lyric.

This unfolding of the self through the missing was a scenario that few had yet considered in personal narrative. Yet it was precisely this composite identity that held both the known and the unseen of a lifetime.

To finally discern how those missing persons defined him, like a spider web defines the spider, was magical. This was the route to magical realism in his life. This was the force that knows grace. This image of the self as spider was a fascination as much as a reality, a glow given off by the living as they die. This gave an available grandeur to his memories while he remained suspended, anxious like a spider before the rain.

This was the new web of relationships that swirled in his old man's mind that day. When he read his own thoughts, the re-porter in him felt that he had made a huge scoop—a cosmic scoop, in fact, as if he had lifted the veil on the other 96 percent. *"Welcome to the dark side,"* he said to himself, smiling. There were still things to discover, thought paths to run through like a deer. Even an old man's teeth can be menacing and satisfied at the same time. He had always loved lifting veils, but this one seemed, at age ninety-six, to matter a great deal.

Each morning, the radiant self asks about the rest of life— which, he believed, could best be concentrated on through writing. And so he dared to write vignettes: a mix of memory, life, and something extra. A passage by Joseph Conrad—another writer with a Polish heritage—in one of his forgotten letters to his family, seemed to have been written just for him:

> *It seems to me I am trying to tell you a dream—making a vain attempt, because no relation of a dream can convey the dream sensation in full, that commingling of absurdity, surprise, and bewilderment in the tremor of a struggling revolt, that notion of being captured by the incredible, which is the very essence of dreams.*

He had transformed his life into a cluster of vignettes: some absurd, some warm and loving, some full of surprise, and some containing a vivid tremor of hope that, when he was lucky, shadowed forth in the suspension that makes us whole.

MEMORY IS
THE ACCOMPLISHMENT

PROFESSOR M. H. ABRAMS, his mentor at Cornell, never really left his world—as Abrams and his larger self had never, even for a day, left the world of Cornell. The professor had successfully converted his physical body into a word body. That is, he found a way to phrase a set of lasting words, a worldview, if you will, that could be passed on to folks like Harold Bloom of Yale, and many others like himself, with little distortion or fabrication. This conversion, this transformation, of the physical self into a social self was the greatest lesson he had learned while at Cornell. It would be done through hard work, and creative persistence. Without first having that example in Abrams—and a few others, like the poet Archie Ammons, also from Goldwin Smith Hall—he might have remained a factory kid, making tools that lasted the test of time, not books.

Almost eight decades ago, when he had first gone walking with Varlissima in Ithaca, Abrams had written something of conclusive, lifelong significance to him: "In thoroughly absorbed contemplation . . . we . . . share the strength, ease, and grace with which a well-proportioned arch appears to support a bridge."

If this was true—if the sublimation of a feeling could be as beautiful and stable as the arch of a building—then Charles Plumer was right! Everything he hoped to convey to his readers was true. He simply had to build the arch that connected him to others like a trembling web.

Lillian Piasecki and Charles Plumer were already long gone from this world, so he walked with his mother in memory, across a set of ancient wooden bridges in Kyoto. In 1988, two months after Lillian had retired from factory work, mother and son traveled to China, Hong Kong, and Japan. It was the most exotic trip he had taken with his mother in this lifetime.

In 2041, with Colette visiting again, he thought of Abrams once more, and wondered whether his daughter was visiting for the last time. In waking the next morning, he continued to write and live this working text with joy, until his sense of an ending began.

It all made sense now; it had turned out the way it was meant to. His longing and his lived experiences, his hopes and his home, were at equilibrium.

The machinery of his memory had worn down, but the machinery of his family would go on.

AROUND HERE, EVERYONE TALKS LIKE LIONS

MANY OF THE PEOPLE HE CAME TO LOVE had rare skills: to know when to stay and when to go.

He always had the ability to love, even after they had left. In the memories of his old age, he never slept alone.

Everyone came to speak like lions so that he could hear them. They spoke with pride, too, as indirection and nuance were weak second cousins to getting through in the first place.

Walt had said, "All goes onwards and upwards, nothing collapses, and to die is different than what anyone supposed, and luckier." An entire zoo of memories filled his mind now, and it was with pride that he looked across that zoo and called it his own.

He remembered the many times when enemies were near—and someone, somehow, kept them from his door. And for this, he felt thanks.

It was now time for him to surrender graciously. Everyone mattered in his pride. Everyone knew it was time. No one told anyone. Everyone just knew it. He honestly took up his voice and threw her to the wind.

Afterword

Five years have passed, and the length of several severe winters, and at last, he sees why writing this book helped him believe in God. Life offers us a few things to learn, then moves on—viciously, like the forty-eight minutes in a basketball game. You can measure life as a stationary set of statistics, and miss it, or enjoy the fast pace.

If we do not learn how to enjoy time-outs, how to breathe in deeply and capture the smell of the cheerleaders, the slant in the stands, and the hopes of the crowd, then we will perish like flapping birds against the glass of a closed stadium.

Poetry, like basketball, is close to force. It gains its force through humor, self-reflection, sportiveness, wit, and a basket of seriousness. Poetry is that same fervor and vigor you can find in your own short life. Poetry boils down to the principles of speed, explosiveness, and the unpredictable—and herein lies its honest and forceful glimpses at eternity.

Poetry, he found, is in Sandy, and her storm; in his mother, and her faith; in Varlissima, and her variety of vivid passions; and in his missing father—if we pause long enough. Sure, you will suffer bruises and burns along the way; sure, you will spin from the contact, and if lucky, complete the shot.

Memoir is not limited to personal narrative; for in its most tender and alert moments, ball in hand, memoir helps us look for our next shot. Open up the floor, spread out the players, and the court of basketball will allow amazing three-point plays, great wealth creation, and supreme entertainment. Keep the game riddled by prejudice and you'll go backwards fast.

It is the same when we believe in God.

Suddenly, there is purpose in our life, commitment to our family. In the election of our ponds, in the sportive contemplation of our captive options in one life, we can see both freedom and fate, friendship and war, brother and sister, believer and nonbeliever. Soon we realize that we are given enough to be able to do more with less.

Open the poem to the vignette, and see grace in action.

But the most important thing to remember is that you must honor the artist within you, even in business, even in family, even when alone.

For if you neglect this gift, life will outpace you.

You sit idle, ball in hand, unable to move forward, unwilling to please the crowd. Without art, without artful thought, without thoughtful action, life becomes a long time-out—which, like a lie, makes the joys of life too short.

About the Author

Bruce Piasecki is the president and founder of AHC Group, Inc., a management consulting firm specializing in energy, materials, and environmental corporate matters. His firm's clients include international companies, as well as a distinct set of leaders in business and society that meet with his team twice a year in a membership-driven Corporate Affiliates Program. Since 1981, he has advised over forty-eight of the Fortune 500 on the critical areas of corporate governance, energy, climate change, environmental strategy, product innovation, and sustainability. He served on Vice President Al Gore's White House Council on Environmental Technology, and was assigned a post under Governor Mario Cuomo as an advisor/researcher for New York State Energy Research and Development.

Dr. Piasecki received his master's degree and doctorate from Cornell University. He was a tenured professor at both Clarkson University and the business school at Rensselaer Polytechnic Institute in Troy, New York. While teaching at Clarkson, he founded the AHC Group in 1981. Dr. Piasecki is the author of ten other books on business strategy, valuation, and corporate change, including the *New York Times* bestseller *Doing More With Less*.

A highly sought-after speaker and educator, Dr. Piasecki offers lectures, workshops, and seminars throughout North America and the world.

For more information regarding the author, visit his website at www.brucepiasecki.com.